THE ULTIMATE GUIDE TO
WOMEN'S FOOTBALL

Published in the UK by Scholastic Children's Books, 2020
Euston House, 24 Eversholt Street, London, NW1 1DB
A division of Scholastic Limited

London ~ New York ~ Toronto ~ Sydney ~ Auckland
Mexico City ~ New Delhi ~ Hong Kong

SCHOLASTIC and associated logos are trademarks and/or
registered trademarks of Scholastic Inc.

Text by Emily Stead © Scholastic Children's Books
Designed by RockJaw Creative for Cloud King Creative

Cover photography © Getty Images

ISBN 978 07023 0204 6

A CIP catalogue record for this book is available from the British Library.

Printed and bound in China.

2 4 6 8 10 9 7 5 3 1

www.scholastic.co.uk

THE ULTIMATE GUIDE TO

WOMEN'S FOOTBALL

SCHOLASTIC

CONTENTS

PLAYER PROFILE

First complete your player profile below.

NAME: ....

BORN: ....

HEIGHT: ....

POSITION: ....

SQUAD NUMBER: ....

THE CLUB I WANT TO PLAY FOR: ....

THE CLUB I SUPPORT: ....

THE COUNTRY I SUPPORT: ....

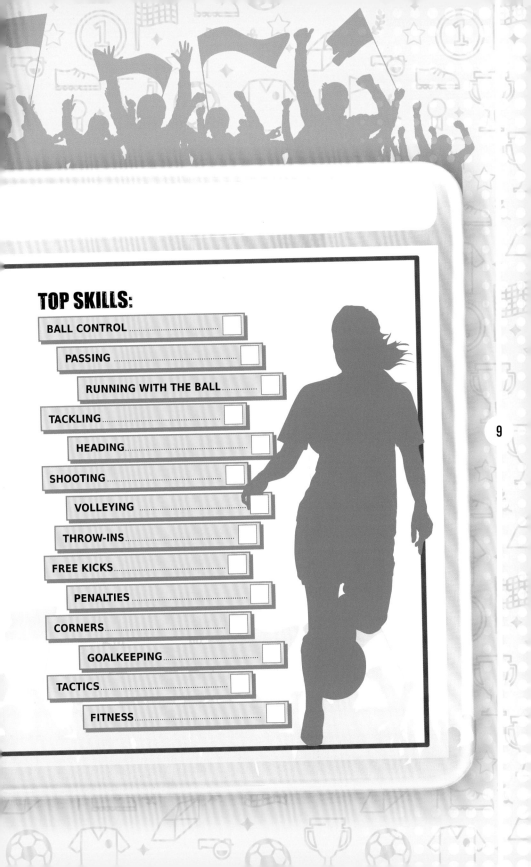

TOP SKILLS:

- BALL CONTROL .... ☐
- PASSING .... ☐
- RUNNING WITH THE BALL .... ☐
- TACKLING .... ☐
- HEADING .... ☐
- SHOOTING .... ☐
- VOLLEYING .... ☐
- THROW-INS .... ☐
- FREE KICKS .... ☐
- PENALTIES .... ☐
- CORNERS .... ☐
- GOALKEEPING .... ☐
- TACTICS .... ☐
- FITNESS .... ☐

A HISTORY OF WOMEN'S FOOTBALL

The history of women's football is very much a game of two halves. While record numbers of women and girls are playing and watching the sport today, females were once banned from playing it altogether in countries such as England, Germany and Brazil. How much do you know about the game's history?

KICKING OFF

Nettie Honeyball (not her real name) is credited with founding the first women's association football club, back in 1894. About 30 young women responded to Nettie's newspaper adverts to recruit players and the British Ladies' Football Club was established a year later. Their first match, played in London, drew a crowd of over 12,000.

In 1914, the First World War broke out across Europe. As thousands of men left to fight overseas, women took on their roles in munition factories and offices. The British government encouraged factories to form women's football teams to keep up morale and to maintain workers' health, as many women worked in hazardous conditions.

12

The Dick, Kerr Ladies team was formed in 1917. Most of its players worked at the factory of the same name in Preston, north-west England. The all-female team soon built a reputation as a skilled and entertaining side and began to draw in huge crowds. On Christmas Day 1917, 10,000 supporters watched the side. By 1920, the team's popularity had soared and on Boxing Day that year, Dick, Kerr Ladies played St Helen's Ladies at a packed Goodison Park in front of 53,000 fans. Thousands more were turned away outside the ground. This set a world record for a women's club fixture that stood for almost a century.

The team's leading scorer was Lily Parr, a strong centre-forward with a wizard of a left foot. Lily played for the Preston side for over 30 years, reportedly scoring close to 1,000 goals.

THE **DICK, KERR LADIES FC** REMAIN ONE OF THE MOST FAMOUS TEAMS IN WOMEN'S FOOTBALL HISTORY.

A HISTORY OF WOMEN'S FOOTBALL

Despite their popularity, the fortunes of the Dick, Kerr Ladies began to change when the First World War ended. At the height of the team's success, the munitions factories closed and women returned to the home. Then in 1921, the English FA (Football Association) delivered a body blow to women's football when they placed a ban on all women's matches being played on their grounds. One FA employee stated:

"THE GAME OF FOOTBALL IS QUITE UNSUITABLE FOR FEMALES AND OUGHT NOT TO BE ENCOURAGED."

It was not until 1971 that the ban in England was lifted (a similar ban in Germany was lifted a year earlier), though it would take decades before the women's game recovered.

GROWING THE GAME

In 1991, the first Women's World Cup was contested in China between 12 nations. The United States were crowned champions, which paved the way for a new professional league to be established back home following the tournament. The WUSA (Women's United Soccer Association) was the world's first women's football league in which all players were paid as professionals. It ran for three seasons before folding, as poor ticket sales and TV ratings failed to make the league profitable. A new league, the WPS (Women's Professional Soccer), ran from 2009–12, before the NWSL (National Women's Soccer League) was founded in 2013.

THE UNITED STATES WON THEIR SECOND FIFA WOMEN'S WORLD CUP IN 1999

In England, the semi-professional FA WSL (Women's Super League) kicked off in 2011. Many players including Kelly Smith and Casey Stoney played in the league while juggling part-time jobs to earn a living.

The 2018–19 WSL season will be remembered as a landmark year for women's football when the league became fully professional for the first time. While its players may still only earn a fraction of the wages paid to male footballers, now girls growing up can aim to have a career in women's football.

MAKING HISTORY

The eighth FIFA Women's World Cup in 2019 was the biggest ever in terms of viewers, prize money and sponsorship. The tournament drew over one billion viewers worldwide, smashing TV records across the globe, including in France, the USA, Germany and China. Almost 59 million people watched Brazil's last-16 game against the host country, France, making it the most watched women's football match of all time.

The United States ran out as champions, earning the biggest share of the $30 million prize fund, though the figure is dwarfed by the $400 million prize money paid to men's teams at the World Cup in 2018.

Despite the huge gap in pay between male and female players, the future of women's football has never looked brighter. The best women's players no longer have to pay to play or wear hand-me-down kits, as they may have done even a decade ago.

More women's games are being shown on TV, and being reported on by the world's media. More tickets are being sold in professional leagues around the globe and, importantly, a new generation of female players is enjoying playing the sport. Women's football may still be playing catch-up to the men's game, but there are glimmers that, one day, the playing field will be equal for all footballers.

MILESTONES IN THE WOMEN'S GAME

1894

Nettie Honeyball advertises in newspapers for players to form a female football team, the British Ladies' FC.

1914

War breaks out across Europe. Thousands of women cover men's positions in factories.

1917

The historic Dick, Kerr Ladies team is formed in a factory in Preston, England.

1996

Women's football is introduced at the 1996 Olympic Games. 76,000 fans see the United States win the gold medal.

1991

The first World Cup is contested by 12 national teams in China. The USA are the champions.

1985

The United States plays its first international match against Italy.

1999

90,185 fans set the attendance record for any women's match at the World Cup final between the USA and China at the Rose Bowl, Pasadena, USA.

2001

WUSA, the world's first professional league for women, is established in the United States.

2011

The first season of the FA Women's Super League (WSL), a semi-professional league, is played in England.

1921
Women are banned from playing on Football League grounds by the English FA.

1955
The German FA bans female membership of its association.

1969
The Women's Football Association is established in England, with 44 clubs.

1971
France v Netherlands becomes the world's first official women's international fixture.

1971
The English FA ends its ban on women's clubs using the grounds of its member clubs.

1970
The German FA lifts its ban on female players, leading to the formation of a women's league the following year.

2019
A record crowd of 60,739 for a women's club fixture see Atlético Madrid v Barcelona, while a global audience of 1.12 billion viewers watch the World Cup.

2020
More women and girls around the world play football than ever before, both professionally and for fun.

PERFECT POSITIONS

A football team is made up of 11 players – ten outfield players and one goalkeeper. Managers can set up their teams in a number of formations depending on how attack-minded or defensively they wish to play. Three substitutes may replace players in any position, for tactical (carefully planned) reasons or if a player becomes injured.

GOALKEEPER

A specialist role within the team, goalkeepers must be agile and good at leaping, catching and kicking. They must stay switched on for the full 90 minutes. Many teams begin their attacks with their keeper, so modern goalies must have excellent footwork too. The keeper is the only player who is allowed to handle the ball on the pitch, but only in their own penalty area.

DEFENDER

From full-backs to central defenders, a defender's job is to prevent the other team from scoring. Blocking shots, intercepting passes, tackling and marking attackers are key responsibilities for defenders. Wing-backs operate slightly further up the pitch and join in their team's attack, but must be ready to defend too, so they need good speed and stamina.

MIDFIELDER

Midfielders are positioned between the defence and the forward line with each type of player tasked with performing a different role. Defensive midfielders protect the team's defence, rarely joining the attack; central midfielders pass the ball to attackers and operate in the middle area of the pitch; attacking midfielders are creative players who provide assists (a play that helps a teammate) for forwards or shoot at goal themselves.

FORWARD

Forwards operate furthest up the pitch and have limited defensive duties. Their main job is to score goals and so often grab the headlines. Centre-forwards and strikers must be clinical finishers (fast and skilled) and strong headers of the ball, aiming to fire as many shots on goal as possible. Wingers can be classed as forwards or midfielders and run up and down the wing, dribbling the ball past defenders into the box or crossing balls into the penalty area for the centre-forwards.

QUIZ: ON THE PITCH

For players that are new to the game, it's sometimes hard to find your best position. Even professionals can change positions during their careers for tactical reasons or to cover injuries or suspensions. Take this quiz to find out where your skills might shine the brightest on the pitch.

1. HOW FAST ARE YOU?

A. My teammates do most of the running..................................

B. I'm about average ....

C. Speed is a big part of my game..................................

D. Catch me if you can! ....

2. HOW SWITCHED ON ARE YOU DURING A MATCH?

A. I don't get many touches, but stay on my guard..................................

B. I constantly track the positions of the opposition ....

C. I'm always alert and looking for the next pass ....

D. I try to be ready to receive the ball..................................

3. HOW GOAL-HUNGRY ARE YOU?

A. Keeping the ball out of the goal is more satisfying for me! ☐

B. As long as my team scores, it doesn't matter whose goal it is ☐

C. Scoring goals is fun, but I love to create chances too ☐

D. I'm all about the goals! I love the glory! ☐

4. WHICH PLAYERS DO YOU MOST ADMIRE?

A. Christine Endler and Sari van Veenendaal ☐

B. Lucy Bronze and Steph Houghton ☐

C. Jordan Nobbs and Megan Rapinoe ☐

D. Ellen White and Alex Morgan ☐

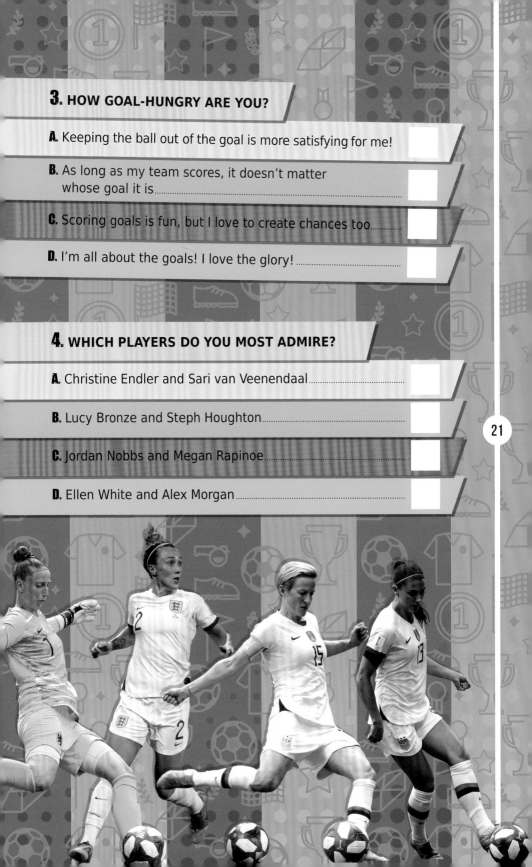

5. WHICH IS YOUR STRONGEST SKILL?

A. My shot stopping...

B. My well-timed tackles ....

C. My pin-point passing ....

D. My eye for goal ....

6. HOW FEARLESS ARE YOU?

A. I throw myself into the action!...

B. I try to block any ball that comes my way..........................

C. I'm not afraid to make a tackle..

D. I'll always attack the ball in the air......................................

7. WHICH NUMBER WOULD YOU PREFER TO WEAR?

A.   **B.**   **C.**   **D.**

1   **5**   **7**   **10**

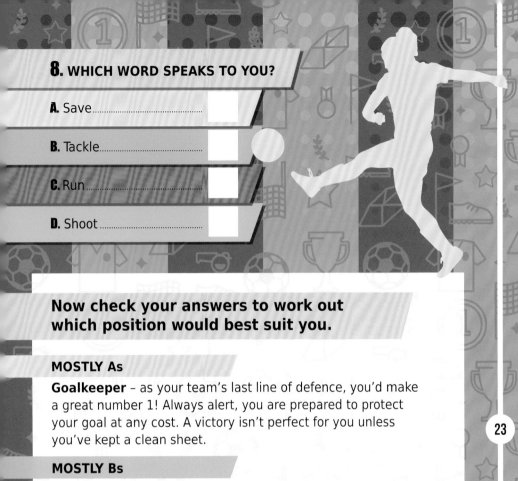

8. WHICH WORD SPEAKS TO YOU?

A. Save...

B. Tackle...

C. Run...

D. Shoot..

Now check your answers to work out which position would best suit you.

MOSTLY As

Goalkeeper – as your team's last line of defence, you'd make a great number 1! Always alert, you are prepared to protect your goal at any cost. A victory isn't perfect for you unless you've kept a clean sheet.

MOSTLY Bs

Defender – naturally defensive, you get more satisfaction from stopping goals from crossing the goal line than scoring them yourself. You're calm under pressure and love nothing better than stealing the ball from a striker.

MOSTLY Cs

Midfielder – you're strong, quick and creative and you pass the ball well. You love to create chances for your teammates and will keep running as the team's midfield engine for the whole 90 minutes.

MOSTLY Ds

Forward – from super strikes to easy tap-ins, your top goal is to get on the scoresheet every time you play. Your hunger for goals and natural attacking flair means you would make a fantastic forward.

WORLD BEATERS

Here are the hotshots, the midfield maestros, the deadly defenders and the no. 1 keepers – twenty players who are currently at the top of their game. Which stars would make your squad? Read all about them, then choose a dream team to take on the world!

1 ....

2 ....

3 ....

4 ....

5 ....

6 ....

7 ....

8 ....

9 ....

10 ....

11 ....

SUBSTITUTES:

12 ....

13 ....

14 ....

15 ....

16 ....

LUCY BRONZE

A brilliant right-back who loves to get forward!

POSITION:	Defender
BORN:	28 October 1991
HEIGHT:	172 cm
CLUB TEAM:	Lyon (France)
NATIONAL TEAM:	England (the Lionesses)
FOOTY FACT:	Lioness Lucy could have chosen to play for Portugal as her dad is Portuguese

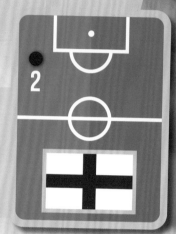

Lucy Bronze is one of the best attacking full-backs in the modern game. She plays her club football for Lyon in France, one of Europe's top teams, and has been an England international since she was 21. Lucy can play anywhere in defence, as well as in midfield, but her strongest position is at right-back. She is an expert tackler (even her middle name is 'Tough'), and loves to attack. Scoring spectacular goals at the biggest tournaments in the world is what Lucy does best!

26

NORTHERN LIGHT

Lucy grew up in the north-east of England and played in a youth team, with and against boys. When she was 12, FA rules meant that she could no longer play in a mixed team and Lucy faced a long drive to train with an all-girls side. Lucy was determined to make it as a footballer, though, and joined Sunderland's academy, signing for the senior side when she turned 16.

LYON'S LIONESS

Lucy suffered some serious knee injuries early on in her career, and worked her way back to fitness to play for some of the best clubs in the Women's Super League. She won the league title with two different teams – Liverpool and Manchester City – before a move to French super club, Lyon. Playing alongside superstars such as Ada Hegerberg and Wendie Renard, Lucy has twice won the Champions League – the top competition for club sides in Europe.

LUCY'S ROCKET RIGHT-FOOT VOLLEY FOR THE **LIONESSES** v NORWAY WAS ONE OF THE GOALS OF THE **2019 WORLD CUP!**

PITCH PERFECT

2019 was a special year for the fantastic full-back, as Lucy's performances on the pitch earned her loads of individual awards. Lucy won the UEFA Women's Player of the Year and the FIFA Women's World Cup Silver Ball, and was named one of the top three players on the planet at the FIFA's Best Women's Player awards. Lucy was humbled and surprised to receive the awards.

CRYSTAL DUNN

A top player who makes any position on the pitch her own!

POSITION:	Defender/Forward
BORN:	3 July 1992
HEIGHT:	157 cm
CLUB TEAM:	North Carolina Courage (USA)
NATIONAL TEAM:	United States (the Stars and Stripes)
FOOTY FACT:	Crystal's sporting hero is tennis legend, Serena Williams

One of the most adaptable players in world football, Crystal can play as a full-back, winger or centre-forward. While forwards Rapinoe and Morgan grabbed the headlines in France, Crystal was the unsung hero of the United States World Cup-winning side. She played in every minute of every match in France, determined to make up for missing out on the 2015 World Cup. The New Yorker is now heading towards 100 appearances for the USA.

KEY PLAYER

Crystal began her senior career with NWSL side, Washington Spirit. In 2015 she won the league's Golden Boot with 15 goals, as well as the Most Valuable Player (MVP), the youngest player to win both prizes at age 23. Her latest club is North Carolina Courage – they reached the NWSL Championship final two years running in 2018 and 2019. Crystal plays in the Courage's midfield, providing goals and assists for the champions.

LONDON CALLING

Crystal spent a season with Chelsea in 2017 in the WSL, an experience she believes improved her as a player. She scored her first goal just 12 minutes into her first competitive appearance for the Blues, and went on to score four more times, featuring 21 times for the club in all competitions. Her time in England was cut short amid fears that she may have lost her place for the national team, but Crystal admits she'd love to play in England again one day. Watch this space!

CRYSTAL IS CONFIDENT SLOTTING IN WHEREVER SHE IS ASKED TO PLAY.

ROLE MODEL

Crystal was just seven when the United States won their second World Cup in 1999 – an event that further put women's football on the map, inspiring a generation of American women and girls to play 'soccer'. But only one non-white player featured in the squad – goalkeeper Brianna Scurry. The current USA squad is more diverse, yet Crystal recognizes the importance of being a strong role model for young people of colour. Every time she steps on to the pitch she tries to lead by example and be the best person that she can be.

CHRISTIANE ENDLER

Chile and PSG's expert penalty-saver!

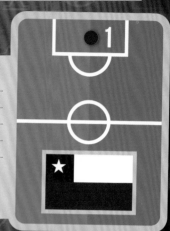

POSITION:	Goalkeeper
BORN:	23 July 1991
HEIGHT:	182 cm
CLUB TEAM:	Paris Saint-Germain (France)
NATIONAL TEAM:	Chile (La Roja)
FOOTY FACT:	Christiane has opened a number of girls-only football schools in her home country, Chile

Captain and goalkeeper for her national side, Christiane is Chile's most-capped player, having represented her country over 70 times (a cap is an international appearance). The team made history in 2019 by making their debut appearance at a World Cup. Although La Roja failed to make it to the round of 16, Christiane's confident displays in goal – particularly against world champions, the USA – earned her plenty of praise, including from retired legendary keeper, Hope Solo.

GAME CHANGER

Everything changed for Christiane when she was 17 and Chile hosted the U-20 (under-20 age team) Women's World Cup in 2008. By this time, she had decided that her best position was as a keeper. Christiane and the team performed well and were treated as professionals. For many in the country, it was the first time they had ever been exposed to women's football. Christiane realized that with hard work and determination, she could turn her talent into a career.

PLAYING FOR KICKS

Christiane credits her older brother with inspiring her love of football, as they often kicked a ball around together growing up. But there was no pathway for girls and women to play football in Chile, and matches were never shown on TV. Christiane grew up not knowing that women's professional football existed around the world. It was only at 16 that she took up the sport, at a German high school she attended. There, her talent was clear, and Christiane developed her skills both in goal and as a striker.

CHRISTIANE'S **INSPIRATIONAL PERFORMANCES** IN FRANCE WON HER MANY FANS.

ON THE MOVE

A short spell with Chelsea in 2014 was blighted by injury and the keeper returned to Chile for two seasons. Her breakthrough season came when Christiane earned a move to Spanish side, Valencia. Competing against top sides, Barcelona and Atlético Madrid, she let in just 11 goals in 30 games. French giants Paris Saint-Germain soon came calling and Christiane became their number 1. Runners-up in the league and Champions League semi-finalists in her first season, she was voted the best goalkeeper in France by her fellow professionals.

PERNILLE HARDER

This Dane is dynamite in front of goal!

POSITION:	Forward
BORN:	15 November 1992
HEIGHT:	168 cm
CLUB TEAM:	Wolfsburg (Germany)
NATIONAL TEAM:	Denmark (De rød-hvide)
FOOTY FACT:	As a young footballer growing up, Pernille's role model was Marta Vieira da Silva

Consistently one of the best players in the world, Pernille is a gifted goalscorer for her Bundesliga (primary football league) club, Wolfsburg, and her country, Denmark. She is an intelligent player with a magical touch and a predator in the box. She has made over 115 appearances for her country and is already the side's second-highest scorer in their history, with her best years still to come.

DREAM COME TRUE

Pernille grew up in a small town in Denmark. Both parents and her elder sister played football and Pernille was keen to follow in their footsteps. She knew, as young as 10, that she wanted to be a professional footballer, and was determined to play her club football in Germany and international football for Denmark. It didn't take the young striker long to realize her dreams as she scored a hat-trick on her international debut, aged just 16.

GOAL MACHINE

A decade on, Pernille captains her country and has played over 115 times for Denmark. An epic scorer, she has over 55 international goals to her name, including three hat-tricks. The country's best performances have come at two European Championships – Euro 2013 and 2017. Denmark surprised many by finishing as runners-up to hosts, the Netherlands, in 2017. However, the Dutch also ended Denmark's dreams of a World Cup place by beating them in the European play-offs.

A YEAR TO REMEMBER

2018 was a stellar year for Pernille. She won the double with her German club and finished as Champions League runners-up. Pernille opened the scoring in extra time, only for Wolfsburg to crumble following Alex Popp's sending off. Despite the loss, Pernille was named the UEFA Player of the Year. Wolfsburg continued their dominance in the German league with another impressive double for the 2018–19 season.

PERNILLE IS THRILLED TO BE A **ROLE MODEL** FOR GIRLS AND BOYS GROWING UP AROUND THE WORLD.

ADA HEGERBERG

An outstanding attacker who has taken the game by storm!

POSITION:	Forward
BORN:	10 July 1995
HEIGHT:	176 cm
CLUB TEAM:	Lyon (France)
NATIONAL TEAM:	Norway (Gresshoppene)
FOOTY FACT:	Ada's elder sister, Andrine, is a midfielder with Italian club, Roma

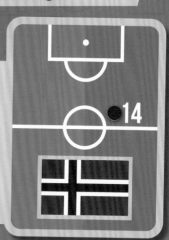

Ada grew up in a small town in Norway, her dad coaching his two daughters until they joined Kolbotn, a top-flight Norwegian team. Even at the young age of 15, Ada was tipped for success – her strong work ethic and desire to score was, and still is, what makes her a special player. A Ballon d'Or winner and European Player of the Year, Ada shines in a team of world-class players at Europe's most successful club side, Lyon. Despite scoring close to 300 career goals and winning over a dozen trophies, Ada strives to improve her game each season.

GROWING REPUTATION

Ada overtook her elder sister Andrine by making her international debut first, as a 16-year-old in 2011. She was also part of the Norway squad that travelled to the 2013 Women's Euro in neighbouring Sweden, scoring her first goal in the quarter-final defeat to Spain. Two years on and Ada exploded on to the global stage by scoring three goals at the 2015 World Cup, her performances earning her a nomination for the tournament's Best Young Player. Just a year later, Ada was awarded the 2015 Norwegian Gold Ball, given to the best footballer in Norway.

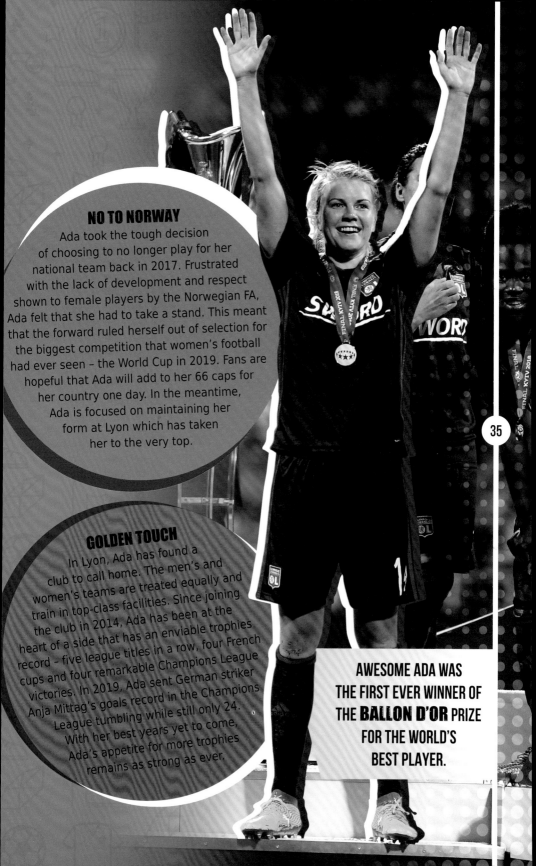

NO TO NORWAY

Ada took the tough decision of choosing to no longer play for her national team back in 2017. Frustrated with the lack of development and respect shown to female players by the Norwegian FA, Ada felt that she had to take a stand. This meant that the forward ruled herself out of selection for the biggest competition that women's football had ever seen – the World Cup in 2019. Fans are hopeful that Ada will add to her 66 caps for her country one day. In the meantime, Ada is focused on maintaining her form at Lyon which has taken her to the very top.

GOLDEN TOUCH

In Lyon, Ada has found a club to call home. The men's and women's teams are treated equally and train in top-class facilities. Since joining the club in 2014, Ada has been at the heart of a side that has an enviable trophies record – five league titles in a row, four French cups and four remarkable Champions League victories. In 2019, Ada sent German striker Anja Mittag's goals record in the Champions League tumbling while still only 24. With her best years yet to come, Ada's appetite for more trophies remains as strong as ever.

AWESOME ADA WAS THE FIRST EVER WINNER OF THE **BALLON D'OR** PRIZE FOR THE WORLD'S BEST PLAYER.

AMANDINE HENRY

France's commanding captain plays with class

POSITION:	Midfielder
BORN:	28 September 1989
HEIGHT:	171 cm
CLUB TEAM:	Lyon (France)
NATIONAL TEAM:	France (Les Bleues)
FOOTY FACT:	Amandine was chosen to captain France ahead of Lyon skipper, Wendie Renard

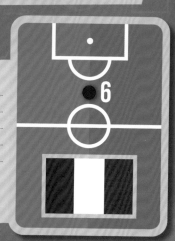

36

The work of a defensive midfielder often goes unnoticed – breaking up the play or winning back possession won't grab the headlines, but Amandine is a player who can do all this and more. Her composure, passing range and ability to lift her team put her among the best midfielders in the world. She also loves to get on the score sheet and is an excellent finisher from outside the box.

EARLY START

Amandine has been inseparable from a ball since the age of five. She played mixed football until she was 13 and began her senior career at 15. A knee injury kept her out of the game for 18 months soon after she joined Lyon, but the midfielder returned to action and began a glittering career in football. The lynchpin of a phenomenal Lyon side, Amandine is into double figures for league titles with the club and has won the Champions League a record five times to date.

AMERICAN ADVENTURE

In 2016, Amandine left Lyon in search of a new challenge. The midfielder had won every trophy going at Lyon, and was keen to experience living abroad and learning a new language. Amandine tried her luck in the NWSL with Portland Thorns and played alongside Tobin Heath and Christine Sinclair to earn more silverware (trophies). A strong season saw the Thorns win the play-offs after finishing the regular season in second place. Amandine returned to Lyon in 2018.

AMANDINE'S **DETERMINATION** AND **ATHLETICISM** HAVE SEEN HER SHINE FOR BOTH LYON AND FRANCE.

INTERNATIONAL RECORD

Amandine helped Les Bleues reach the quarter-finals at the World Cup 2015 in Canada, where her own commanding performances saw her win the tournament's Silver Ball. At the 2019 World Cup on home soil, Amandine scored a stunning goal in the group stages, but France failed to progress beyond the quarter-finals, when they came up against the unstoppable United States. Amandine's next goal is to lead France at the UEFA Women's Euro in 2021.

STEPH HOUGHTON

The super skipper of City and the Lionesses!

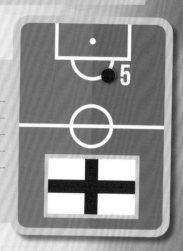

POSITION:	Defender
BORN:	23 April 1988
HEIGHT:	174 cm
CLUB TEAM:	Manchester City (England)
NATIONAL TEAM:	England (the Lionesses)
FOOTY FACT:	Steph played alongside Lioness Jill Scott as a Sunderland schoolgirl

38

England and Manchester City captain Steph leads by example and is hugely honoured to captain her country. The unflappable centre-back soaks up the pressure on the pitch and is an inspirational role model for any young player wanting to get into the game. Her timely tackles and famous free-kicks have seen Steph become one of the finest defenders in the women's game in England.

DETERMINED DEFENDER

Steph's first England call-up came as a 17-year-old in 2007, a World Cup year. Sadly though, a broken leg ended her hopes of making the World Cup squad and a second serious injury prevented her from playing at Euro 2009. The defender had to wait until the London 2012 Olympics to make a name for herself, when her three goals from her left-back position shot her to fame. Since then, Steph's inner steel has driven her to win over 100 caps for the Lionesses, and she has captained the side to two World Cup semi-finals in 2015 and 2019.

GLORIOUS GUNNER

In three excellent seasons as an Arsenal player between 2010 and 2013, Steph added six trophies to the FA Women's Cup she had won with Leeds. Arsenal (the Gunners) also reached the Champions League semi-finals three times in a row, with Steph a key cog in defence. It was during her time in London that Steph was also handed the captain's armband for England, an honour that surprised but delighted the defender.

STEPH STARTED OUT AS
A **STRIKER** AND HAS
SCORED SOME SCREAMERS
OVER THE YEARS.

CITY CHALLENGE

When the WSL expanded in 2013, Steph switched clubs from Arsenal to newcomers, Manchester City. Steph was made captain and she has never looked back. Five cups and a league title in 2016 – when City went unbeaten in the league for a whole season – justified her move north. A first Champions League title would be the icing on the cake for a player who is respected throughout football.

SAM KERR

The Matildas' goal machine waltzes past defenders with ease!

POSITION:	Forward
BORN:	10 September 1993
HEIGHT:	167 cm
CLUB TEAM:	Chelsea (England)
NATIONAL TEAM:	Australia (the Matildas)
FOOTY FACT:	For several seasons, Sam split her time playing in both the US and Australian leagues

With pace to burn, laser-guided shooting and a heroic heading ability, Sam Kerr is Australia's high-flying striker. She has topped the scoring charts season after season in the NWSL and Australia's W-League, earning her multiple nominations for FIFA's Best Women's Player and Ballon d'Or awards. In international football, Sam has made over 80 appearances for the Matildas and has her sights set on breaking Australia's all-time scoring record.

SOCCER SWITCH

Sam grew up in Western Australia, playing Aussie-rules football, a rugby-like sport. Both her father and brother played professionally and Sam showed a great talent for the game too, outsprinting most boys on the pitch. But by the age of 12, the boys had grown bigger and the game became too rough. Heartbroken at having to leave the sport, Sam reinvented herself as a footballer, and at 15 earned her first cap for Australia.

WORLD STAGE

Although still only in her mid-twenties, the 2019 tournament was Sam's third World Cup. The ruthless striker led by example in France, wearing the captain's armband with pride and scoring five goals to take the Matildas to the knockout stages. She became the first Australian to score a World Cup hat-trick with her four goals against Jamaica in the group stage, as Australia finished ahead of Brazil.

LOOK OUT FOR SAM'S SPECIAL **GOAL CELEBRATION** – A SPECTACULAR BACKFLIP WORTHY OF AN OLYMPIC GYMNAST!

LEAGUE LEADER

Sam has played for a trio of clubs in the American NWSL. She holds the record for the league's all-time top scorer with 77 goals and was named the league's Most Valuable Player in 2019, after scoring a record 18 goals in 21 games – while missing part of the season because of the World Cup. Having shone in America and Australia, Sam moved to Chelsea in January 2020 to test herself on a new stage in Europe's top league, the WSL.

MARTA VIEIRA DA SILVA

Megastar Marta has magic in her feet!

POSITION:	Forward
BORN:	19 February 1986
HEIGHT:	162 cm
CLUB TEAM:	Orlando Pride (USA)
NATIONAL TEAM:	Brazil (As Canarinhas)
FOOTY FACT:	Having spent a decade playing in Sweden, Marta was granted Swedish citizenship in 2017

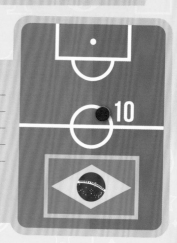

Brazilian forward Marta has had a magical career in football. Her goals, stylish play and leadership have seen her crowned World Player of the Year an amazing six times. At the 2019 World Cup (her fifth), Marta wrote her name in the record books by scoring a record 17th tournament goal – no player has scored more World Cup goals, male or female. Marta is quite simply a legend.

BRAZIL HEARTACHE

While Marta has won almost every individual honour in the game, Brazil's captain has experienced heartache with her country. Brazil came closest to winning the World Cup in 2007 when they finished as runners-up to Germany. That year, Marta became the first female to win both the Golden Boot and Golden Ball at the same World Cup tournament. Marta also has two Olympic silver medals from the Games in 2004 and 2008 as Brazil lost both finals in extra time.

SHOWING COURAGE

As well as breaking records, Marta has had to smash stereotypes in her rise to the top of women's football. Marta grew up in one of Brazil's poorest towns at a time when girls were scorned for wanting to play football (it was actually illegal for women and girls to play the game in Brazil between 1941 and 1979). Marta's passion for the game was so great that she left her family and her home at 14 to follow her dream, moving first to Rio de Janeiro and later to Sweden while she was still a teenager.

MARTA HAS SCORED MORE GOALS (17) AT **WORLD CUP FINALS** THAN ANY OTHER PLAYER — MALE OR FEMALE.

NEXT GEN

Following her country's exit from the World Cup in 2019, Marta made an emotional plea to the next generation of players in Brazil to help push forward the women's game back home. With a lack of young talent waiting to replace a host of Brazil stars coming to the end of their careers (including herself, Formiga and Cristiane), Marta appealed to girls to train harder and step up to continue their legacy.

LIEKE MARTENS

Left-winger Lieke has loads of tricks in her locker!

POSITION:	Forward
BORN:	16 December 1992
HEIGHT:	170 cm
CLUB TEAM:	Barcelona (Spain)
NATIONAL TEAM:	Netherlands (Oranje)
FOOTY FACT:	Lieke is regularly shortlisted for the top prizes in women's football

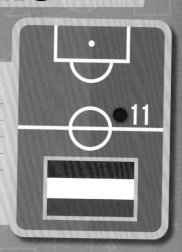

44

Lieke become a hero in her home country of the Netherlands after a series of fine performances fired the Oranje to their first UEFA European Championships on home soil in 2017. The Dutch forward claimed the Golden Ball for the tournament's best player and in the same year Lieke was named the Best FIFA Women's Player for 2017. She plays her domestic football for Barcelona, the club of her childhood hero, the long-haired winger, Ronaldinho.

LAST LAUGH

Lieke grew up in a tiny village in the Netherlands, not knowing that a women's national team even existed in her country. She was never without her beloved football, and was the only girl in a boys' junior side until the age of 16. Many people used to scoff when Lieke told them of her dream to become a professional footballer, but the forward has since had the last laugh. At 15, Lieke left home to join up with the Netherlands under-19 side and, despite having to grow up quickly, has never looked back.

AWAY FROM HOME

Her professional career began with Heerenveen in the Dutch top flight as a teenager and before long Lieke had tasted life in Belgium, Germany and Sweden's premier leagues. Then in July 2017, Lieke signed for Barcelona. She remains one of few foreign players at the Spanish club. The forward helped Barcelona reach their first Champions League final in 2019 and is contracted to play in Catalonia until 2022.

RAPID RISE

Lieke has been a key player in the Dutch side which has been on a fairytale journey to the top of women's football. With over 100 caps and over 40 goals to her name, Lieke was a member of the Netherlands' first World Cup squad in 2015, and again four years later as the dazzling Dutch side reached the World Cup final. Tokyo 2020 will be the Netherlands' first appearance at an Olympic Games where Lieke and her team will be going for gold.

HAVING GROWN UP WITHOUT ANY **FEMALE ROLE MODELS** IN FOOTBALL, LIEKE LOVES INSPIRING YOUNG GIRLS TO GET INVOLVED IN THE GAME.

VIVIANNE MIEDEMA

A sensational striker who's smashed every goals record going!

POSITION:	Forward
BORN:	15 July 1996
HEIGHT:	175 cm
CLUB TEAM:	Arsenal (England)
NATIONAL TEAM:	Netherlands (Oranje)
FOOTY FACT:	Vivanne's advice to female players is to play against boys for as long as possible

Arsenal's super striker Vivianne Miedema plays with a maturity beyond her years. From a football-loving family based in the north of the Netherlands, she has trained since she was a toddler. She began her senior career as a 14-year-old schoolgirl playing against grown women for Heerenveen and was a full international by 17. At 22, she had already scored more international goals than any other player - male or female - in Dutch history.

MUNICH MOVE

When Bayern Munich were interested in bringing Vivianne to the Bundesliga, the then 18-year-old striker jumped at the opportunity, moving to Germany without being able to speak a word of the language. In her first seasons with Bayern, they were a young side that claimed back-to-back titles in a league that, at the time, was the strongest in the world. Then in 2017, Vivianne joined the WSL club, Arsenal, the club of her childhood hero, Netherland's forward, Robin van Persie.

EURO HERO

On the international stage, Vivianne was a part of the unfancied Netherlands' team that won the home UEFA Women's Euro 2017. Her four goals in the tournament, including two in a thrilling final against Denmark, saw the Dutch win the trophy for the first time, sending their fans wild. The team built on its success by reaching the 2019 World Cup final. Vivianne may now be an icon at home in the Netherlands, but she remains a modest player. Letting her feet do the talking is the secret to this striker's success.

WSL WONDER

Vivianne soon settled into an Arsenal side that included Netherlands' attacker Daniëlle van de Donk. The tall striker's next achievement was to finish the season as the WSL's top scorer, with a record 22 goals scored. Her haul for the season was an incredible 39 in 46 games in all competitions as the Gunners were crowned 2018–19 league champions. Her feats were rewarded when her fellow players voted Vivianne PFA Player of the Year.

VIVIANNE IS A TWO-FOOTED STRIKER AND LETHAL FINISHER.

ALEX MORGAN

An American girl with a golden touch!

POSITION:	Forward
BORN:	2 July 1989
HEIGHT:	170 cm
CLUB TEAM:	Orlando Pride (USA)
NATIONAL TEAM:	United States (the Stars and Stripes)
FOOTY FACT:	In October 2019, Alex announced that she and her partner were expecting their first child

13

Forward Alex is the poster girl for the United States national team, having burst on to the scene at the 2011 World Cup, when she scored in the semi-final and again in the final, despite being the youngest player in the squad. Her current appearances for the United States women's national soccer team stand at 169, while she has scored 107 goals and made 43 assists – a phenomenal contribution to her team's success on the world stage.

ALEX'S JOURNEY

Alex grew up in California, and shone in a number of sports, particularly sprinting. She didn't start playing football competitively until her early teens. At high school, Alex was scouted for the Olympic Development Program and starred for her college side, the University of California's Golden Bears. Her professional career kicked off in 2011 where she won the championship with Western New York Flash, before adding a second league title to her honours in 2013 with Portland Thorns. She now partners Marta in Orlando Pride's attack.

CRUCIAL GOALS

Injury may have delayed her first call-up to the national side, but since making her USA debut in 2010, Alex has been at the heart of the USA's progress at every major tournament. Following the 2011 World Cup, Alex was again the hero at the London 2012 Olympic Games. Her dramatic extra-time header in the 123rd minute of the semi-final against Canada took the USA to the gold medal match, which they went on to win. Back-to-back World Cup wins followed in 2015 and 2019.

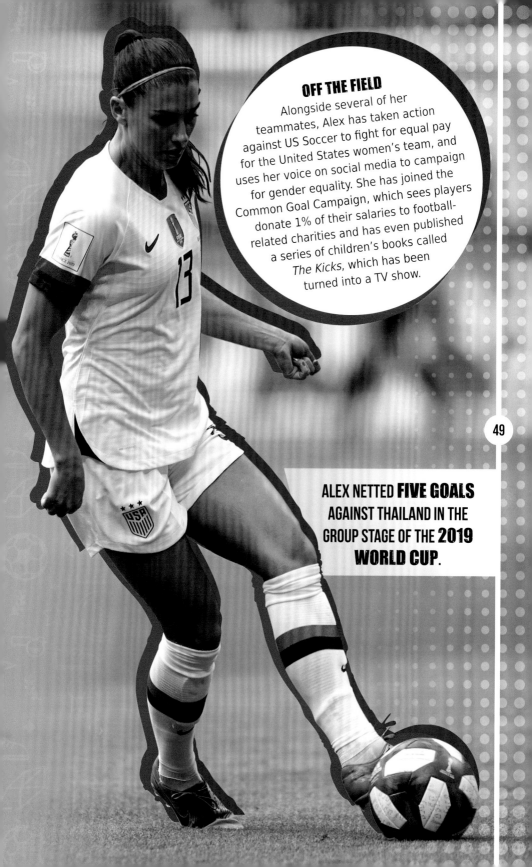

OFF THE FIELD

Alongside several of her teammates, Alex has taken action against US Soccer to fight for equal pay for the United States women's team, and uses her voice on social media to campaign for gender equality. She has joined the Common Goal Campaign, which sees players donate 1% of their salaries to football-related charities and has even published a series of children's books called *The Kicks*, which has been turned into a TV show.

ALEX NETTED FIVE GOALS AGAINST THAILAND IN THE GROUP STAGE OF THE 2019 WORLD CUP.

JORDAN NOBBS

This creative midfielder loves to shoot from long range

POSITION:	Midfielder
BORN:	8 December 1992
HEIGHT:	160 cm
CLUB TEAM:	Arsenal (England)
NATIONAL TEAM:	England (the Lionesses)
FOOTY FACT:	Jordan met fellow Lioness Demi Stokes when they were eight and nine, while on a trial with Sunderland. Over 15 years later, they are still playing together!

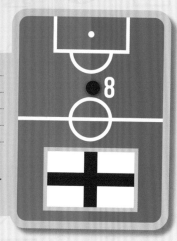

50

Arsenal's midfield dynamo and England's vice-captain, Jordan is a special player with the ability to influence games from the centre of midfield. A small player, she has excellent technique and vision, and is a fierce competitor in every game in which she features. Some of her best performances have come on big occasions, when Jordan has stepped up to deliver important goals for her team.

EARLY PROMISE

Another Lioness who grew up in the north-east of England, Jordan was kicking a ball around with her dad (a former lower-league professional) as soon as she could walk. Growing up, she relished showing off her skills against boys' teams every Saturday morning. Jordan joined Sunderland's academy aged eight, and was playing in the first team by the age of 16. Her performances earned her a move to champions Arsenal, when the WSL was formed.

INJURY SETBACK

Jordan was left heartbroken when a serious injury ended her dream of playing in a second World Cup in France. The injury to her anterior cruciate ligament came at a time when the midfielder was in the best form of her career and would have been one of the first picks for the Lionesses. After nine and a half months of tough rehab, Jordan scored with her first shot on her comeback, a WSL match against rivals Spurs.

JORDAN HAD TO SIT OUT THE 2019 WORLD CUP WITH A SERIOUS **KNEE INJURY**, BUT WORKED AT THE TOURNAMENT AS A TV PUNDIT AND MAGAZINE COLUMNIST.

51

FAN FAVOURITE

Jordan has now been at Arsenal for a whole decade and loves the London club just as much as the fans love her. She's won a century of caps for Arsenal since 2010 as well as a host of major trophies, including the WSL three times. Only the Champions League title is missing from her collection.

NIKITA PARRIS

This free-scoring forward is a danger to any defence!

POSITION:	Forward
BORN:	10 March 1994
HEIGHT:	162 cm
CLUB TEAM:	Lyon (France)
NATIONAL TEAM:	England (the Lionesses)
FOOTY FACT:	Nikita's older sister Natasha Jonas was a professional boxer

An epic goalscorer from a young age, right-footed Nikita combines pace with excellent finishing. Her natural eye for goal has seen her represent the Lionesses senior team from the age of 20. Her first England goals came in her second match and Nikita has since reached double figures for international goals, finishing as the team's top scorer in World Cup qualifying.

52

CITY STAY

The young forward moved to City (the Sky Blues) on a season-long loan in 2015, which would later be made permanent. Nikita's time with City was a success, as the team claimed the WSL title in 2016, two FA Cups and two League Cups. Her 19 WSL goals for City in 2019 also saw Nikita named the Football Writers' Association Footballer of the Year. The attacker contributed 62 goals in 127 in all appearances with the club.

TOFFEES TEENAGER

Nikita joined Everton (the Toffees) at the age of 14, making her senior debut for the club in the Champions League at 16. Despite the forward scoring 11 goals in 19 games in her first WSL season with the Toffees, Everton failed to win a league match and were relegated to the second tier. Keen to continue her progress and put herself in contention for a place in the England senior team, Nikita made the switch to Manchester City.

FRENCH TEST

Just after the World Cup had kicked off in 2019, French and European Champions Lyon announced that they were taking Parris to France on a three-year contract. The forward joined Lionesses teammate Lucy Bronze at the club. Having scored on her league debut, Nikita's biggest challenge is to hold down a regular place in Lyon's fantastically talented attack.

BEFORE LEAVING FOR LYON, NIKITA WAS THE TOP SCORER IN WSL HISTORY.

MEGAN RAPINOE

The United States' wondrous wing wizard!

POSITION:	Midfielder
BORN:	5 July 1985
HEIGHT:	168 cm
CLUB TEAM:	Seattle Reign (USA)
NATIONAL TEAM:	United States (the Stars and Stripes)
FOOTY FACT:	Megan once scored directly from a corner at the London 2012 Olympic Games!

15

Megan Rapinoe is a clever winger who never fails to put in a performance on the biggest stages. Her exploits at the World Cup earned the USA a record fourth trophy, while Megan herself claimed the Golden Ball and Golden Boot for the tournament's best player and top scorer. Her stunning international form saw her later named the Best FIFA Women's Player for 2019 ahead of teammate Alex Morgan.

FOOTBALL FAMILY

Megan grew up in rural California, one of six siblings. Inspired by her elder brother, Megan and her twin sister Rachael (who also played professionally) took up football at the age of three. Coached by her dad until high school, Megan developed into a creative attacking player who loved to assist just as much as getting on the scoresheet. At college, she suffered two knee injuries while playing for the University of Portland Pirates, which helped to shape Megan's mental strength.

54

MEGAN IS ONLY THE SECOND PLAYER TO HAVE WON BOTH THE GOLDEN BOOT AND GOLDEN BALL IN THE SAME WORLD CUP.

WORLD'S BEST

Megan has been one of the United States' leading players as the team has dominated world football over the past decade. Her glittering career on the left wing has seen her win the World Cup in 2015 and 2019 along with the Olympic gold medal at London 2012. In all, she has 160 caps for her country and has reached a half-century of international goals. An inspirational player, Megan will be much missed when the time comes for her to hang up her boots.

MEGAN'S REIGN

Most of Megan's career has been spent playing in America's top domestic league, the NWSL (formerly WPS). Starting out with Chicago Red Stars, the winger has played for five different US clubs and spent time abroad at Sydney FC in Australia and Lyon in France. Captain Megan has starred for Reign FC in Seattle since 2013, winning the NWSL Shield twice, and can count Brits Jodie Taylor and Jess Fishlock among her teammates.

WENDIE RENARD

France and Lyon's rock in the centre of defence

POSITION:	Defender
BORN:	20 July 1990
HEIGHT:	187 cm
CLUB TEAM:	Lyon (France)
NATIONAL TEAM:	France (Les Bleues)
FOOTY FACT:	Wendie often played football with a plastic bottle growing up, on the beach or in a car park

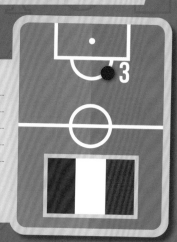

56

Standing tall at 187 cm, Wendie has been a colossal talent for club and country, playing for France at three World Cups and two Olympic Games, while helping Lyon to dominate club football in Europe for over a decade. Her cool defensive play and towering headers in both boxes have seen the defender earn over a century of caps for Les Bleues. She's an expert penalty-taker and influential captain too.

DREAMING BIG

Born on the French island of Martinique in the Caribbean, it was the women in the Renard family who encouraged a young Wendie to play football – even though she was the only girl who joined in. Wendie was football obsessed and watched every match she could when she wasn't playing. At 14, Wendie had a successful trial with Lyon in France and moved thousands of miles from home to follow her dream of becoming a professional footballer.

LYON'S LEADER

Wendie plays in the heart of Lyon's defence and is one of the most decorated players in the history of women's football. Since joining the club in 2006, Wendie is close to claiming a staggering 30 major trophies, including eight Champions League titles and 13 French league championships, many of these won with Wendie captaining the squad of superstars.

PLAYING AT HOME

Wendie played every minute of France's World Cup campaign in 2019 on home soil. Her four goals – one a coolly retaken penalty – helped Les Bleues reach the quarter-finals. Sadly for Wendie, France lost to the reigning champions, the USA, although the defender still has ambitions to win a major tournament with her country. Having missed out on a spot at the 2020 Olympics, France's next chance to challenge for silverware will be at Euro 2021.

WENDIE IS ONE OF THE **MOST DECORATED FOOTBALLERS** IN THE WORLD.

CHRISTINE SINCLAIR

Canada's legendary goal queen shows that class is permanent

POSITION:	Forward
BORN:	12 June 1983
HEIGHT:	175 cm
CLUB TEAM:	Portland Thorns (USA)
NATIONAL TEAM:	Canada (CANWNT)
FOOTY FACT:	Christine once featured on a stamp to celebrate the 2015 World Cup in Canada!

13

58

Canada's courageous captain and top goalscorer will be remembered as one of the greatest female footballers of all time. Fast, strong and ever-hungry to get on the scoresheet, Christine can be relied upon to come up with the goals on the biggest of occasions. In January 2020, the striker set a new world record for international goals scored by any man or woman – an outstanding 185 strikes.

RECORD OF SUCCESS

Christine was offered a scholarship at Portland University in 2001 and excelled playing college football in the United States, recording 110 goals and 32 assists for the Pirates. Since making her professional debut, Christine has won four championships with three teams in the United States – Gold Pride, Western New York Flash and most recently with her current club, Portland Thorns in 2013 and 2017. She has been nominated for FIFA's World Player of the Year seven times during an outstanding 20-year career in football.

FAST-TRACKED

Born and raised in British Colombia, Canada, Christine grew up in a footballing family, her father and uncles all playing the sport. She showed great promise in basketball and baseball as a youngster, but football won out, as Christine was blessed with the bug for scoring goals. Her progress in the game was rapid, and Christine was picked for Canada's senior squad at the age of 16. That year, she opened her international goal-scoring account scoring an incredible 15 goals in her first 18 appearances for Canada. She has remained a first pick ever since.

CHRISTINE IS ONE OF ONLY TWO WOMEN TO HAVE SCORED IN **FIVE** DIFFERENT WORLD CUPS – **INCREDIBLE!**

CLASS ACT

Christine can count two Olympic bronze medals among her biggest achievements for Canada, won at the 2012 and 2016 Games. At London 2012, the striker bagged the Golden Boot trophy with six goals, registering a hat-trick against the United States. As she approaches the end of her career, Christine shows few signs of slowing down. The world record for international goals scored would be a fitting tribute to a player who has been at the top of her game for two decades.

DANIËLLE VAN DE DONK

A versatile player who brings quality and goals in midfield

POSITION:	Forward
BORN:	5 August 1991
HEIGHT:	160 cm
CLUB TEAM:	Arsenal (England)
NATIONAL TEAM:	Netherlands (Oranje)
FOOTY FACT:	Daniëlle's best friend in football is Netherlands teammate, Lieke Martens

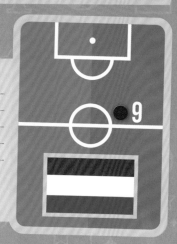

Attacking midfielder Daniëlle delights Arsenal and Dutch fans with her top tricks and sensational goals. She's been an influential player for club and country, collecting a stack of silverware with the Gunners, while winning the Euro 2017 title and finishing as World Cup 2019 runners-up with the Netherlands. She celebrated her 100th international cap in October 2019 and has scored over 20 international goals to date, including two hat-tricks.

CHAMPION SPIRIT

Arsenal signed a special talent in the shape of the attacking midfielder in 2015, with Alex Scott, Casey Stoney and Kelly Smith all welcoming Daniëlle to the London club. She has felt at home ever since, and has helped the Gunners win three trophies, including the WSL Championship in 2018–2019, while playing in a number of roles on the pitch. Netherlands teammates and fellow attackers Vivianne Miedema and Jill Roord have since joined the club too.

ON THE MOVE

Like many of her fellow footballers, Daniëlle started young, playing football from the age of four and crediting playing against boys with helping to strengthen her game. She began her professional career as a teenager in the Dutch top flight, the Eredivisie, and played for three different clubs. Her third club, PSV Eindhoven was the club she had grown up supporting. Daniëlle spent three seasons there, impressing with a goal-scoring streak of 30 goals in 53 appearances.

DANIËLLE WAS A KEY MEMBER OF THE DUTCH 2019 WORLD CUP SQUAD, PLAYING **EVERY MINUTE** OF THE FINAL.

MEMORABLE MATCHES

Winning the Euro 2017 final against Denmark on home soil was a game-changer for Daniëlle and her Dutch teammates. The team sparked a football revolution, with the players becoming overnight celebrities in the Netherlands. The tournament is one of Daniëlle's proudest achievements in football. The team's rapid rise to the top of world football continued in 2019, as the Netherlands reached their first World Cup final, with some stunning displays along the way. Beaten finalists, the Tokyo 2020 Olympics will be the Dutch side's next chance to shine.

SARI VAN VEENENDAAL

She's the girl with the golden gloves!

POSITION:	Goalkeeper
BORN:	3 April 1990
HEIGHT:	177 cm
CLUB TEAM:	Atlético Madrid (Spain)
NATIONAL TEAM:	Netherlands (Oranje)
FOOTY FACT:	Perfectionist Sari is frequently the last player to leave the training pitch

62

Sari has long been one of the best keepers in the women's game. The captain of the Netherlands side that reached the 2019 World Cup final, her shot-stopping, fast reflexes and composure on the ball have seen her join the ranks of the world's elite goalkeepers. Two awards in 2019 – the Golden Glove at the World Cup and the Best FIFA Women's Goalkeeper topped off a fantastic year.

LATE START

Sari discovered her talent for football much later than many of her teammates – it wasn't until she was 17 that she began playing at a high level. Sari admits that a lack of female role models in football growing up may have played a part in her late introduction to the sport. Today, the landscape is much brighter and Sari is thrilled to be regarded as a hero, inspiring many young footballers in her home country and around the world.

CLUB FOOTBALL

After going pro in 2007, Sari spent eight years learning her trade as a goalkeeper with FC Utrecht and FC Twente. A move to English club Arsenal came in 2015, by which time she had worn the Netherlands' number 1 shirt at Euro 2013 and the World Cup in Canada that summer. Her time in London was a success – Sari won three trophies with Arsenal, but left in search of a new challenge in 2019, having lost her place to Pauline Peyraud-Magnin in the Gunners' goal. Spanish side Atlético Madrid was her next destination.

SARI IS AS COMFORTABLE WITH THE BALL **AT HER FEET** AS SHE IS AT **CATCHING** AND **THROWING.**

WORLD'S NO. 1

Some of the best performances in Sari's career came when the Netherlands won Euro 2017 on home soil. Sari conceded just three goals in the entire tournament as her Dutch side finished as surprise winners. Two years later, Sari captained the Netherlands to their first World Cup final in France. The keeper shone in the final, making a string of impressive saves against the United States. While Sari was unlucky to be on the losing side, her performances earned her the Golden Glove award for the tournament's best keeper.

ELLEN WHITE

A super striker with a brilliant goal celebration to boot!

POSITION:	Forward
BORN:	9 May 1989
HEIGHT:	170 cm
CLUB TEAM:	Manchester City (England)
NATIONAL TEAM:	England (the Lionesses)
FOOTY FACT:	Ellen is a West Ham United fan and tries to catch the men's matches when she's not playing herself

At five years old, Ellen started playing at her father's football academy. She was never afraid to take on boys who were bigger and stronger than she was, including her elder brother. When she signed to Arsenal's academy aged eight, it was clear that Ellen's love affair with football was set to last – she was always the first to training and had to be dragged off the pitch at the end of each session. Ellen has gone on to become one of the highest-scoring English forwards ever.

64

SUPER SIX

Manchester City is the sixth English club that Ellen has represented in a successful career in football so far, with some injury setbacks along the way. Her move back to childhood club Arsenal in 2010 was where the striker won six major trophies, including back-to-back WSL titles. Her summer 2019 switch to Manchester City robbed Birmingham City of their top scorer – a cool 23 goals in 26 games – though reunited Ellen with England teammates, Steph Houghton and Keira Walsh.

EXPERIENCED ELLEN

Ellen has represented her country for a whole decade – at three World Cups, two Women's Euros and at the London 2012 Olympic Games (with Team GB). She is England's top scorer in the current squad, as well as the fifth highest-scoring Lioness of all time. Ellen's dream is to reach a century of caps with England, which is not far from the striker's reach.

ELLEN WAS SHORTLISTED FOR THE PRESTIGIOUS WOMEN'S **BALLON D'OR** PRIZE FOR THE FIRST TIME IN 2019.

WORLD CUP WONDER

Ellen was in the form of her life at the World Cup in France, as her goal streak helped England to reach the semi-finals. Her trademark 'goggles' celebration became known around the world! The forward came close to scoring seven times, but her goal against the USA was heartbreakingly ruled out for offside. Had the goal stood, Ellen would have won the Golden Boot trophy ahead of Megan Rapinoe and Alex Morgan.

TOP TROPHIES

Teams and players are remembered by the trophies that they win. The world of women's football has many respected prizes on offer that can be claimed at top international knockout competitions or by finishing first after a challenging league season. Read about the most wanted trophies in the game across the globe.

FIFA WOMEN'S WORLD CUP

The greatest prize in women's international football is undoubtedly the Women's World Cup. Organized by FIFA, the tournament has been held every four years since 1991. Teams from across the globe compete in the finals in a month-long competition to decide the world champion.

RECORD BREAKERS

Over 1 billion viewers tuned in to the official broadcast coverage of the World Cup 2019 – a record audience for the competition. The final match between the United States and the Netherlands attracted a total of over 260 million unique viewers, as the USA claimed a record fourth title. With live coverage reaching more countries than ever before, it is hoped that many more women and girls will be inspired to play the game.

YEAR	HOSTS		CHAMPIONS	
1991		China		United States
1995		Sweden		Norway
1999		United States		United States
2003		United States		Germany
2007		China		Germany
2011		Germany		Japan
2015		Canada		United States
2019		France		United States

GLOBAL GAME

Of the 144 nations from around the world that entered qualification, 24 teams made the World Cup finals at France 2019. Norway and Germany are the only European nations to have won the competition, while the USA and Japan complete the list of champions. FIFA hope to keep growing the women's game globally by extending the 2023 edition of the World Cup to feature 32 teams.

69

THE UNITED STATES CELEBRATE BACK-TO-BACK TITLES AFTER VICTORIES AT CANADA 2015 AND FRANCE 2019.

TOP TROPHIES: FIFA WOMEN'S WORLD CUP

As well as the famous World Cup trophy awarded to the winning team, players are rewarded for their individual performances throughout the tournament. No woman has won the coveted Golden Boot or Golden Ball more than once in World Cup history.

BEST PLAYERS

The three players who impress on the pitch throughout the tournament are awarded the Golden, Silver and Bronze Ball trophies. Megan Rapinoe, Lucy Bronze and Rose Lavelle's performances were judged to have been the best at France 2019.

YOUNG STAR

FIFA's Young Player Award recognizes the best performances by a player who is 21 or younger. The 2019 World Cup was only the third time the prize had been awarded, this time to Germany midfielder, Giulia Gwinn. Canada's Kadeisha Buchanan won at Canada 2015, while Australia's Caitlin Foord won the award in 2011 when she was just 16.

GIULIA HELPED GERMANY TO REACH THE **QUARTER-FINALS** IN FRANCE.

USA'S **MEGAN RAPINOE** WAS NAMED THE **BEST PLAYER** AND **TOP SCORER** AT FRANCE 2019, WINNING THE **GOLDEN BALL** AND **GOLDEN BOOT** TROPHIES ALONGSIDE HER **WORLD CUP** WINNERS' MEDAL.

TOP SCORERS

The Golden, Silver and Bronze Boots are awarded to the highest-scoring players in the competition. Although three players shared the same goals tally in France – Megan Rapinoe, Alex Morgan and Ellen White, Megan scored her six goals in fewer minutes.

GOLDEN GLOVE

The Golden Glove trophy recognizes the technical performances of goalkeepers. Netherlands number 1, Sari van Veenendaal, won the award for keeping three clean sheets as her outstanding saves took the Dutch side all the way to the final. USA legend Hope Solo is the only goalie to have twice won the Golden Glove.

FIFA Women's World Cup France 2019™ adidas

WOMEN'S FOOTBALL AT THE OLYMPIC GAMES

Women's football has been contested at the summer Olympic Games since 1996. Before the Games in Tokyo 2020, only three different nations had ever won Olympic gold – the United States along with European sides, Norway and Germany.

GOING FOR GOLD

Female players of any age can play in the competition, a knockout tournament that features 12 teams. The first women's tournament was held at the 1996 Atlanta Games and was won by hosts, the USA. The Stars and Stripes have since claimed three further gold medals, most recently at London 2012. Brazil forward Cristiane is the tournament's record goalscorer.

72

GERMANY OVERCAME FINALISTS SWEDEN 2–1 AT THE RIO 2016 OLYMPIC GAMES.

Fill in the three medal-winning teams at the Tokyo 2020 Olympic Games below.

....
....

....
....

....
....

TOKYO 2020

The top three performing European teams at the World Cup 2019 earned their spot at Tokyo 2020 – Great Britain (through England's performance), Netherlands and Sweden. Team GB can choose players from England, Scotland, Wales and Northern Ireland. Japan qualify as hosts and Brazil will be determined to impress, having narrowly missed out on a medal in Rio. Teams from North and South America, Oceania, Africa and Asia complete the 12 sides.

IF SELECTED, **BRAZIL'S FORMIGA** COULD APPEAR IN AN **INCREDIBLE** SEVENTH **OLYMPIC GAMES**.

UEFA WOMEN'S EURO

The European Championships for women, also called the Women's Euro is organized by UEFA. Contested every four years, the summer tournament decides the champion nation of Europe.

COMPETITION HISTORY

The first winners of the championships were Sweden in 1984, when they beat in England by a single strike in a penalty shoot-out. Germany have had the most success in the competition, winning the Euro an impressive eight times, including a winning streak of six titles in a row between 1995 and 2013.

ROAD TO WEMBLEY

The 2021 tournament will be held in England, with Wembley Stadium in London hosting the final. 16 teams will play in stadiums across the country from Manchester United's ground Leigh Sports Village in the north of England to Brighton & Hove Albion's Community Stadium in the south. Hundreds of thousands of fans will be able to see some of the world's best players in action, while millions more are expected to watch the televised tournament globally.

TITLE DEFENDERS

Defending champions and World Cup finalists Netherlands will be one of the favourites to be Euro heroes in 2021. The Oranje's first title was won in 2017, when they beat Denmark 4–2. Winger Lieke Martens was named the best player of the tournament, scoring three goals, including one in the final.

LIEKE MARTENS (FRONT ROW, SECOND FROM LEFT) WILL BE 28 AND AT THE PEAK OF HER CAREER IN 2021.

FINAL

Lyon, France
07.07.2019

WOMEN'S SUPER LEAGUE

The Women's Super League (WSL) is the top league in England. Its first season kicked off in 2011, and 12 clubs compete in a league to try to become English champions each year. Matches are action-packed and teams boast some of the world's top players, as the league turned fully professional for the 2018–19 season.

THE BIG FOUR

Four different clubs have won the WSL since 2011 – Arsenal, Liverpool, Chelsea and Manchester City – though newly formed teams like Manchester United could be title contenders before too long.

GOING PRO

It is only in the last decade or so that women's football in England turned professional, meaning that most players in the WSL no longer have to juggle a job with matches and training. Former England legend Kelly Smith had to pay to play football when she started out, while both she and Lucy Bronze had jobs at fast-food restaurants while they played for top clubs.

ARSENAL WERE CROWNED **WSL CHAMPIONS** IN 2019.

GUNNERS' FORWARD
VIVIANNE MIEDEMA
HAS SCORED THE
MOST WSL GOALS IN
A SINGLE CAMPAIGN – **22**
IN THE 2018–19 SEASON.

GROWING THE GAME

Thanks to a growing appetite
for women's football, matches
were streamed live – and for free – for
the first time so fans could catch every
minute of the 2019-20 season. More WSL
matches were covered live on the radio,
too. Clubs hope to attract more fans than
ever before, investing profits from
ticket sales back into the women's
game. Why not grab a ticket
and go see your heroes
in action?

CUP COMPETITIONS

The two major cup competitions in England are the FA Women's Cup and the FA Women's League Cup. With plenty of drama, cup finals have often gone to extra time or nail-biting penalty shoot-outs to decide which team takes home the silverware.

FA WOMEN'S CUP

Teams first competed for the prestigious FA Cup in 1970, when Southampton ran out the victors. The Saints went on to dominate the competition in the 1970s, winning the trophy seven times in a row, while Arsenal love this cup competition – they've won the trophy an incredible 14 times. In 2015, the final was played at Wembley Stadium for the first time and attracted a record crowd of 30,710 fans.

MANCHESTER CITY WERE THE **FA CUP** WINNERS IN 2019, BEATING WEST HAM UNITED 3—0 AT WEMBLEY.

FA WOMEN'S LEAGUE CUP

The League Cup is sometimes called the 'Conti Cup', thanks to its sponsors, Continental Tyres. The first edition of the cup was played in 2011, when Arsenal claimed the trophy as part of a famous treble with the league championship and FA Cup. So far, only Arsenal and Manchester City have won the League Cup, with unlucky Birmingham City finishing as runners-up three times.

ARSENAL ARE THE ONLY TEAM TO HAVE WON THE LEAGUE CUP **THREE TIMES IN A ROW**, BETWEEN 2011 AND 2013.

UEFA WOMEN'S CHAMPIONS LEAGUE

The UEFA Women's Champions League is an annual tournament in which the top club sides in Europe compete for glory. It was first staged in 2001, when it was called the UEFA Women's Cup. The final is played in the same city that hosts the men's Champions League final.

QUALIFICATION

Clubs can qualify for the competition by finishing as champions or runners-up in their domestic league. Each of the top eight leagues in Europe is awarded two places. Unlike the men's competition, which includes group stages, the women's format is a knock-out tournament. Ties are played over two legs until the final, which is a single match.

RECORD BREAKERS

French side Lyon have been European champions more times than any other club (six). Their talented squad boasts many of Europe's top players – England stars Lucy Bronze, Nikita Parris and Alex Greenwood have all crossed the channel to join the French champions. Lyon's Norwegian-born forward Ada Hegerberg holds the record for the most goals ever scored in the history of the Champions League, claiming the record at the age of just 24.

MARTA ONCE SCORED A GOAL AFTER ONLY **12 SECONDS** FOR UMEÅ IN THE **CHAMPIONS LEAGUE FINAL** OF 2008 (FIRST LEG)!

NATIONAL WOMEN'S SOCCER LEAGUE

The National Women's Soccer League (NWSL) is the premier league in the United States. Its first season officially began in 2013, although a professional league has operated in the USA since 2001. Nine teams from across America bid to become league champions in front of crowds of up to 25,000 fans.

SEATTLE REIGN

PORTLAND THORNS

UTAH ROYALS

BIG LEAGUE

Each of the nine teams plays 24 games over the regular season, 12 at home and 12 away. Teams play each other three times. Unlike in England, there aren't many local derbies – a fixture between Portland Thorns and Orlando Pride means the away club has to travel over 3,000 miles!

COMPETITION FORMAT

At the end of the 'regular season', the top four teams in the NWSL play off to decide the champion. The top team plays the team that finished fourth, while second and third go head to head. Play-off matches cannot be drawn, so extra time and penalties are used if needed.

WORLD STARS

In addition to the entire USA World Cup squad playing in the NWSL, including Megan Rapinoe and Tobin Heath, the league attracts some of the most talented players in women's football. Marta, Christine Sinclair and Lioness Rachel Daly all currently star for US clubs, while Kelly Smith, Amandine Henry and Sam Kerr have also crossed the pond to appear in the NWSL.

SAM KERR REMAINS THE NWSL'S TOP SCORER OF ALL TIME AND HOLDS THE RECORD FOR THE MOST GOALS SCORED IN A SEASON — **18 STRIKES IN 24 GAMES**.

SKY BLUE

WASHINGTON SPIRIT

CHICAGO RED STARS

CAROLINA COURAGE

HOUSTON DASH

ORLANDO PRIDE

GOLDEN GREATS

Women's football has seen plenty of highs and lows over the past 100 years or so, with many legends of the modern game having to overcome prejudice and poor pay and conditions during their careers. Read the profiles of ten trail-blazing players who helped to put women's football on the map, inspiring generations of women and girls to put on their boots.

MICHELLE AKERS

One of the greatest attackers to have graced the women's game!

POSITION:	Forward/Midfielder
BORN:	1 February 1966
NATIONAL TEAM:	United States
TROPHY HIGHLIGHTS:	World Cup Winner (1991, 1999), Olympic Gold (1996)
FOOTY FACT:	Michelle originally wanted to play American football, but there was no pathway in the game for girls to play the sport

Michelle was a warrior for the USA in the 1990s. Her strength and long stride made her the perfect striker, earning her over 100 goals. She was the star of the first ever Women's World Cup in 1991, striking twice in the final to beat Norway 2-1. Illness forced Michelle to switch to a defensive midfield role towards the end of her career, a position she also made her own.

NADINE ANGERER

A German goalkeeper who enjoyed a glittering career!

POSITION:	Goalkeeper
BORN:	10 November 1978
NATIONAL TEAM:	Germany
TROPHY HIGHLIGHTS:	World Cup winner (2003, 2007), European Championships winner (1997, 2001, 2005, 2009, 2013)
FOOTY FACT:	In 2014, Nadine became the first keeper (male or female) to be named FIFA World Player of the Year

87

This golden goalkeeper stepped up when it counted to lead her team to victory on some of the world's biggest stages. Nadine's special skill was saving vital penalties, including one from Marta in the 2007 World Cup final. She was a part of a brilliant German side that won two World Cups and five fantastic UEFA Women's Euros.

MIA HAMM

Winner of two World Cups and two Olympic gold medals!

POSITION:	Forward/Midfielder
BORN:	17 March 1972
NATIONAL TEAM:	United States
TROPHY HIGHLIGHTS:	World Cup Winner (1991, 1999), Olympic Gold (1996, 2004), Olympic Silver (2000)
FOOTY FACT:	Mia now runs a foundation to help give young girls opportunities to play sport

Twice named FIFA's World Player of the Year, Mia is remembered as the first global superstar of women's football. Speed, creativity and technique were among her best attributes on the pitch and in front of goal, she was one of the greatest ever finishers. Mia made her international debut at 15 in 1987, and starred 275 times for the United States, scoring a then world-record 158 goals.

KRISTINE LILLY

This record-breaking star is nicknamed the 'Queen of Caps'!

POSITION:	Forward/Midfielder
BORN:	22 July 1971
NATIONAL TEAM:	United States
TROPHY HIGHLIGHTS:	World Cup winner (1991, 1999), Olympic Gold (1996, 2004), Olympic Silver (2000)
FOOTY FACT:	Kristine is one of only nine women to play in five World Cup tournaments

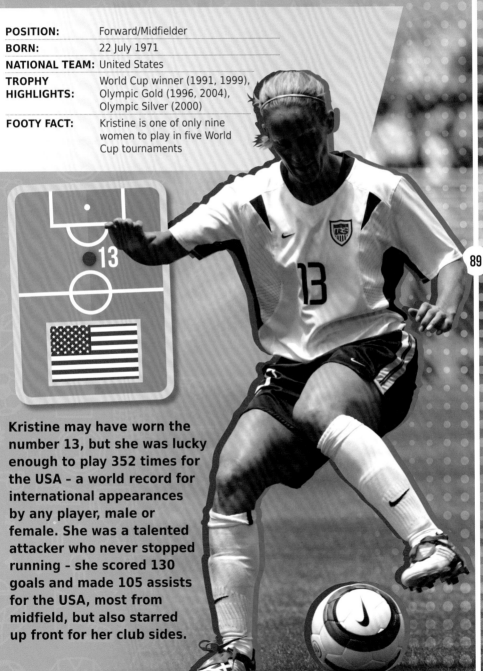

13

89

Kristine may have worn the number 13, but she was lucky enough to play 352 times for the USA - a world record for international appearances by any player, male or female. She was a talented attacker who never stopped running - she scored 130 goals and made 105 assists for the USA, most from midfield, but also starred up front for her club sides.

BIRGIT PRINZ

Germany's number 9 was terrifically talented!

POSITION:	Forward
BORN:	25 October 1977
NATIONAL TEAM:	Germany
TROPHY HIGHLIGHTS:	World Cup winner (2003, 2007), Olympic Gold (2016), European Championships (1995, 1997, 2001, 2005, 2009)
FOOTY FACT:	Birgit was once approached to play for Italian club Perugia – for the men's first team!

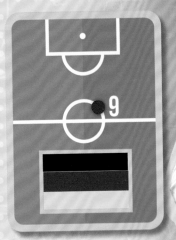

Simply unstoppable in front of goal, no one could stop the shots of this powerful German forward. Birgit played over 200 times for her country, scoring 128 goals – 14 of these at World Cup tournaments. She became a legend for Germany at the most successful time in their history, winning the World Cup twice and five UEFA Women's Euros.

HEGE RIISE

Norway's natural-born winner!

POSITION:	Midfielder
BORN:	18 July 1969
NATIONAL TEAM:	Norway
TROPHY HIGHLIGHTS:	European Championships (1993), World Cup winner (1995), Olympic Gold (2000)
FOOTY FACT:	Hege is one of only three women in the world to win the Olympics, the World Cup and the Women's Euro

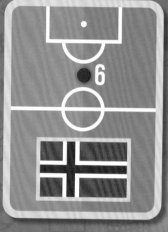

One of the first real playmakers in the women's game, the Norwegian ran the midfield for every team in which she played. Hege's vision and creativity helped Norway to win their only World Cup in 1995, where she was named the tournament's best player. An Olympic Gold at Sydney 2000 and winning the Women's Euro with Norway in 1993 were also among the highlights of her special career.

HOMARE SAWA

Considered by many to be the best Asian player of all time

POSITION:	Midfielder
BORN:	6 September 1978
NATIONAL TEAM:	Japan
TROPHY HIGHLIGHTS:	World Cup winner (2011), Olympic Silver (2012)
FOOTY FACT:	Homare won the Golden Boot and the Golden Ball at the 2011 World Cup

Homare exploded on to the scene aged 15, when she scored four for Japan on her debut. She had already played in Japan's top league at 12! Homare went on to play for Japan over 200 times during a 23-year international career. She proudly captained Japan to their first World Cup victory in 2011, as the Asian side beat the USA in a tense penalty shoot-out.

KELLY SMITH

A special striker and record goalscorer!

POSITION:	Forward
BORN:	29 October 1978
NATIONAL TEAM:	England
TROPHY HIGHLIGHTS:	Four English league titles (1996–97, 2005–06, 2006–07, 2007–08), UEFA Women's Cup (2006–07)
FOOTY FACT:	Kelly represented Team GB at the London 2012 Olympics where the team reached the quarter-finals

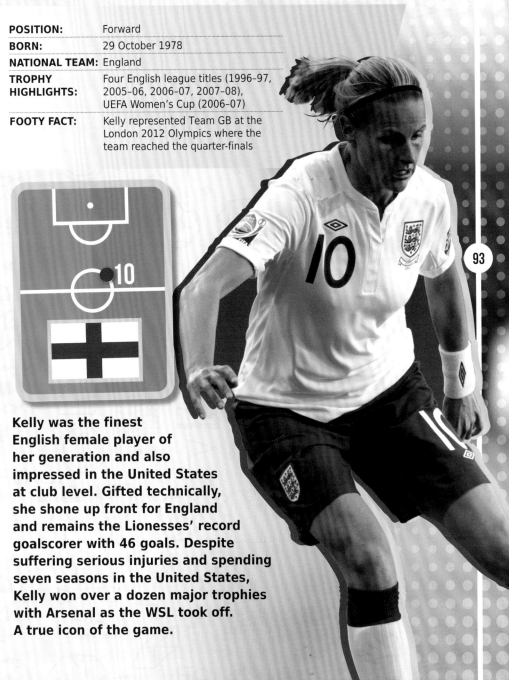

93

Kelly was the finest English female player of her generation and also impressed in the United States at club level. Gifted technically, she shone up front for England and remains the Lionesses' record goalscorer with 46 goals. Despite suffering serious injuries and spending seven seasons in the United States, Kelly won over a dozen major trophies with Arsenal as the WSL took off. A true icon of the game.

HOPE SOLO

America's legendary keeper with golden gloves!

POSITION:	Goalkeeper
BORN:	30 July 1981
NATIONAL TEAM:	United States
TROPHY HIGHLIGHTS:	World Cup winner (2015), World Cup runner-up (2011), Olympic Gold (2008, 2012)
FOOTY FACT:	Hope played as a striker while at high school and scored over 100 goals! Wow!

94

Hope was a simply awesome shot-stopper who always played with passion. Her excellent positioning and quick reflexes allowed her to pull off some jaw-dropping saves and she was the first female goalkeeper to keep 100 international clean sheets. Hope twice won the Golden Glove Award at the World Cups in 2011 and 2015 for the tournaments' best goalkeeper and boasts two Olympic gold medals among her list of honours.

ABBY WAMBACH

An outstanding player and golden goalscorer!

POSITION:	Forward
BORN:	2 June 1980
NATIONAL TEAM:	United States
TROPHY HIGHLIGHTS:	World Cup winner (2015), World Cup runner-up (2011), Olympic Gold (2004, 2012)
FOOTY FACT:	Abby became known for her goals scored from athletic diving headers

95

Only a few chosen players in football can claim to be a G.O.A.T. but Abby is certainly among the Greatest of All Time! A strong, athletic forward, Abby scored goals for fun, racking up a world-record 184 strikes for the United States, and earning her a World Cup winners' medal in 2015, as well as two Olympic golds.

WONDER WOMEN

As the women's game grows, records are being created and smashed every season. Here are just some of the amazing feats achieved by female footballers and their fans in recent seasons, from bumper attendances to jaw-dropping scorelines! These World Cup records all have the wow factor...

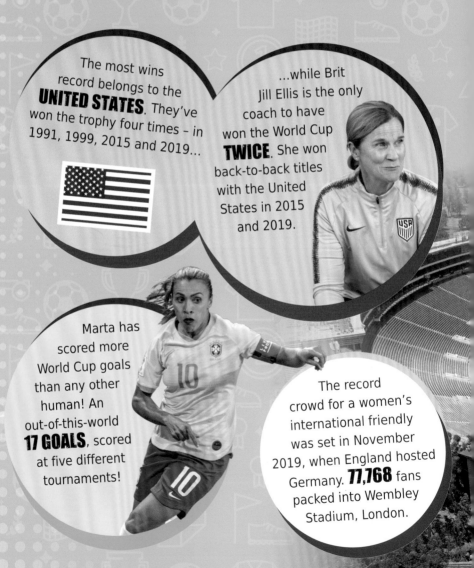

The most wins record belongs to the **UNITED STATES**. They've won the trophy four times – in 1991, 1999, 2015 and 2019...

...while Brit Jill Ellis is the only coach to have won the World Cup **TWICE**. She won back-to-back titles with the United States in 2015 and 2019.

Marta has scored more World Cup goals than any other human! An out-of-this-world **17 GOALS**, scored at five different tournaments!

The record crowd for a women's international friendly was set in November 2019, when England hosted Germany. **77,768** fans packed into Wembley Stadium, London.

The United States' **13–0** record thrashing of Thailand at the 2019 World Cup is a scoreline that may never be bettered at the tournament!

Brazil midfielder Formiga is the only player (male or female) to have played at **SEVEN** World Cups! Wow!

Formiga is also the oldest female to have played in a World Cup – she was **41 YEARS AND 112 DAYS** young when Brazil faced France in 2019!

The record attendance for a women's match still stands at **90,185** – when the United States took on China in the 1999 World Cup final. The match took place at the Rose Bowl, Pasadena, USA.

An incredible **1.12 BILLION** viewers tuned into official broadcast coverage of the 2019 World Cup across all platforms – a record audience for the competition.

...while these records set in club football around the world will take some beating! Share the stats and facts that follow to impress your teammates!

Megastar Marta once scored **103 GOALS** in just **111** games for Swedish side **UMEÅ IK**, a record any player would give their right boot to have set!

In a WSL match in 2019, Dutch predator Vivianne Miedema scored a record **6** goals and made **4** assists. Not bad for **70** minutes on the pitch!

43,264 fans set the record attendance for a Women's FA Cup final in 2019 as Manchester City beat West Ham United 3-0 under Wembley's famous arch.

98

ARSENAL have an enviable trophies record – to date, they've won more trophies than any other English women's club, including the league 15 times, the FA Cup 14 times and the Champions League once.

Aussie goal machine Sam Kerr is the **ALL-TIME TOP SCORER** in two different leagues, thousands of miles apart – America's NWSL (69 goals) and Australia's W-League (70 goals)!

The record crowd for a match in the English Women's Super League was smashed in November 2019 when **38,262** watched the North London derby between Spurs and Chelsea at the Tottenham Hotspur Stadium.

Paris Saint-Germain's evergreen forward Formiga is the **OLDEST GOALSCORER** in Champions League history – at 41 years and 193 days young!

French club Lyon hold the record for the most **CHAMPIONS LEAGUE TITLES** (six)...

...while their forward, Ada Hegerberg is the top scorer in the history of the competition! She was also the first ever female winner of the **BALLON D'OR** trophy in 2018.

PRO SKILLS

If you're dreaming of becoming a pro footballer or just want to be the best player you can be, you'll need to be prepared to work hard to develop your skills. Every player that features in this book is football obsessed and has put in hour after hour, just themselves and a ball, to improve their technique. Read on to learn how to master the basic skills and take your game to the next level.

CONTROL THE BALL LIKE...
ADA HEGERBERG

Being truly comfortable on the ball takes practice, practice and more practice. Develop your touch by juggling the ball on your own. The more touches you take, the better your ball control will be in a match. Use all parts of the body: head, chest, thighs and both feet – not just your dominant foot. Before long, you'll be a baller, just like Ada!

1. Stay on your toes and be ready to adjust your body position.

2. Move towards the ball to control it early, aiming for a good first touch.

3. Move into the line of flight of the ball keeping your head up and your eyes fixed on it.

4. Decide which part of the body should make contact with the ball (foot, head, thigh or chest) and relax the surface area so that you can cushion the ball to fall exactly where you want it.

5. Be aware of teammates and opponents and where they are positioned to determine your next move, which you should decide before you receive the ball. Could you fire a shot on goal, dribble down the pitch or pass to a better-placed teammate?

102

RUN WITH THE BALL LIKE...
LIEKE MARTENS

Dazzling dribbler Lieke has the tekkers (skills) and the confidence to run past defenders without losing possession of the ball. Mastering running with the ball takes hours of practice, but all you need is a football and an open space to get started. Follow the tips below to improve your dribbling.

1. Keep the ball close to your feet and take quick, light touches as you move it. If you're running into space, you can make a stronger connection.

2. Moving the ball with your laces (instep) will help you dribble faster, but use the outside or inside of your foot to turn and change direction. Take touches with both feet to improve your dribbling.

3. To help your balance, keep your arms out and your knees bent to a create a low centre of gravity.

4. Try to keep your head up, so you can see where your teammates and opponents are positioned.

5. Use your body to shield the ball when a defender approaches.

6. Accelerate past defenders with a quick burst of speed.

PASS THE BALL LIKE...
JORDAN NOBBS

Passing the ball is a basic skill that every footballer should try to master. Lioness and top Gunner Jordan Nobbs is one player capable of delivering a killer pass that leads to a goal. From short balls to long-range crosses, here are two techniques to deliver pinpoint passes to your teammates, just like Jordan.

SHORT PASSING

Use your sidefoot (inside of the foot) to make a short pass. This technique doesn't generate the most power, but it provides greater accuracy to find a teammate who's close to you.

1. Approach the ball at an angle of about 30 degrees, keeping your eyes on the ball and using your arms for balance.
2. Plant your non-kicking foot close to the side of the ball, keeping your ankle firm.
3. Swing through with your kicking leg, aiming to strike the centre of the ball with the side of your foot.

LONG PASSING

1. Longer passes are used to find a teammate in space or switch play quickly.
2. Approach the ball as you would for a short pass, but this time, strike the centre of the ball with your laces (instep), with your toes pointing downwards.
3. Lean back a little to get lift on the ball.
4. Follow through with your kicking leg to increase the power behind the pass, keeping your knee behind the ball.

SHOOT LIKE...
ELLEN WHITE

Lionesses' leading striker Ellen White scored the most goals from open play at the World Cup in 2019 (jointly with Alex Morgan). Whenever she had the opportunity to shoot, Ellen confidently snapped up her chances. Follow these important tips to help you make every shot count.

1. When a chance falls to you, quickly check where the keeper is positioned – have they left a gap?

2. Choose the best technique for you – shooting with your instep (laces) will give you power, while a side-foot shot will provide greater accuracy.

3. Plant your non-kicking foot alongside the ball, keep your body over the ball, your head down and your eyes on the ball.

4. Aim to make contact with the middle or top half of the ball, striking the ball cleanly.

5. Shooting low along the ground makes it harder for a goalkeeper to reach. A shot across the keeper is tougher for them to handle, meaning the ball could fall into the path of an attacking teammate.

6. Try to stay composed and imagine your strike hitting the back of the net.

HEAD THE BALL LIKE...
WENDIE RENARD

Towering defenders like Lyon and France's Wendie Renard make heading the ball look easy, but you don't need to be super tall to head the ball well ... it's about timing your jump and making contact with the correct part of the ball.

DEFENSIVE HEADERS

When making a defensive header, direct the ball with your head away from your goal and up into the air. To head upwards, use your forehead to make contact with the underside of the ball. As the ball approaches in the air, position yourself in line with it. Then jump to head the ball, aiming to make contact at the highest point of the jump to get the most height and distance.

ATTACKING HEADERS

If you get a chance to head the ball at goal from within the penalty box or six-yard box, try to direct the ball with your head downwards towards goal. Leap above the incoming ball and make contact with the top half of the football, trying to generate as much power as you can.

USE A SOFT BALL WHEN PRACTISING YOUR HEADERS.

VOLLEY THE BALL LIKE...
LUCY BRONZE

Not the easiest skill to master, right-back Lucy Bronze has scored some spectacular volleys for the Lionesses. Keep your eyes on the ball and aim to make a clean connection while the ball is in the air and before it drops to the ground.

To perform the volley technique...

1. Angle your hips in the direction you want the ball to go, then plant your standing foot in the same direction – towards your target.

2. Try to connect with your laces, aiming for as close to the middle of the ball as possible for the cleanest strike.

3. Wait until the ball drops to the perfect height – too high and you'll sky it over the bar, too low and you'll drive the ball into the ground.

4. Keep your head and chest over the ball and use your arms for balance. Swing through with your kicking foot in the direction of the target.

TACKLE LIKE...
STEPH HOUGHTON

Tackling is used to win possession of the ball from the opposition. Top defenders like Steph Houghton stop attackers in their tracks, taking the ball safely for their team without giving away a foul. A tackle can be made anywhere on the pitch, so check out these tips whatever your position.

1. Stay light on your toes and keep your eyes on the ball at all times.

2. Stay close (about one metre or so) to your opponent, and stay patient until the opportunity to make a tackle presents itself. Sometimes just staying close to an opponent forces them to make a mistake.

3. With your ankle locked, use the inside of your foot to make a firm connection with the centre of the ball and win the ball cleanly.

4. Commit to the tackle fully and stay on your feet after you've made contact with the ball.

5. Move away with the ball and look to make a pass to a teammate.

NEVER TACKLE FROM BEHIND – YOU COULD INJURE YOUR OPPONENT AND RISK RECEIVING A RED CARD.

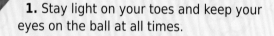

TAKE A PENALTY LIKE...
MEGAN RAPINOE

Three of Megan Rapinoe's six Golden Boot goals at the World Cup were scored from the penalty spot, as the winger remained ice-cool with the world watching. To take the perfect penalty, stay focused and calm, pick a spot and don't change your mind. Believe that you'll score!

1. Place the ball yourself on the penalty spot, making sure it's clear of any bumps in the playing surface. Take a run up of about three or four steps – whatever feels the most comfortable for you.

2. Plant your non-kicking foot to the side of the ball and drive through it with the laces (instep) of your kicking leg. This will give you power, giving the keeper less time to make a save. Follow through with your kicking leg.

3. Decide where you want the ball to hit the back of the net and stick to it. To create height, lean over the ball and plant your foot just behind it. To keep your strike low on the ground, drive hard through the ball. Shots aimed at the top corners are harder to save, but require greater accuracy.

YOUNG STARS

Meet a new generation of players who are taking the world by storm - top teenagers and young players with a bright future in the game. Some have already won silverware or tasted Champions League action, while others have played in a World Cup. You heard about them here first!

ELLIE BRAZIL

This Braz-illiant forward is one to watch!

POSITION:	Forward
BORN:	10 January 1999
CLUB TEAM:	Brighton & Hove Albion (England)
NATIONAL TEAM:	England U-21
FOOTY FACT:	Ellie spent a season playing abroad for Fiorentina in Italy's Serie A

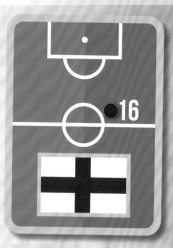

Ellie was on the books at Derby County before she signed for Birmingham City at 16. She could have been a professional athlete, but comes from a footballing family. Ellie then switched countries and spent a season abroad with Italian Serie A club, Fiorentina, where she improved her game. She's now back in the WSL with Hope Powell's Brighton.

ELLIE CARPENTER

An awesome defender who loves to go on the attack!

POSITION:	Defender
BORN:	28 April 2000
CLUB TEAM:	Portland Thorns (USA)
NATIONAL TEAM:	Australia
FOOTY FACT:	Ellie plays her club football over 12,000 miles from her home in Canberra, Australia

By the time she turned 18, Ellie had already smashed loads of records - playing for Australia at 15, becoming the youngest Australian to compete at an Olympic Games, as well as being the youngest player to appear in a NSWL match in America. Athletic Ellie loves to get up and down the wing and is strong in attack, as well as defence.

ERIN CUTHBERT

A Scottish starlet who shines for club and country

POSITION:	Midfielder
BORN:	18 July 1998
CLUB TEAM:	Chelsea (England)
NATIONAL TEAM:	Scotland
FOOTY FACT:	Erin first began playing football as soon as she could walk!

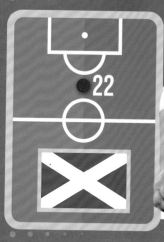

114

Erin was one of the top performers for Scotland as they made their bow at the World Cup finals in 2019. Her goal against Argentina came agonizingly close to helping the Scots reach the knockout stages. The mini midfielder plays her club football for Chelsea and has twice won the WSL with the Blues.

JACYNTA GALABADAARACHCHI

West Ham's wizarding wonder from Oz

POSITION:	Forward
BORN:	6 June 2001
CLUB TEAM:	West Ham United (England)
NATIONAL TEAM:	Australia
FOOTY FACT:	Jacynta's long surname comes from her dad's Sri Lankan roots

West Ham's teenage forward is a handful for defenders and a mouthful for commentators! The Aussie's surname is so long, it wouldn't fit on her shirt, so she wears 'Jacynta' instead. Growing up, Jacynta dreamed of playing football in England and now shows off her attacking skills with the Hammers.

GIULIA GWINN

A speedy midfielder who can operate down either wing

POSITION:	Midfielder
BORN:	2 July 1999
CLUB TEAM:	Bayern Munich (Germany)
NATIONAL TEAM:	Germany
FOOTY FACT:	Giulia played mixed football until she was 16, which she believes helped to make her a stronger player

116

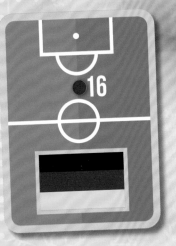

The youngest of four siblings, Giulia began her senior career at the age of 16 with German club, Freiburg. She is a full international for her country too - Giulia had a terrific tournament for Germany at the 2019 World Cup where she was named the best young player in the world. She now plays her club football with Bayern Munich and hopes to win the Champions League one day with the club.

LAUREN HEMP

A young Lioness who's hungry for success

POSITION:	Forward
BORN:	7 August 2000
CLUB TEAM:	Manchester City (England)
NATIONAL TEAM:	England
FOOTY FACT:	Lauren may be a Sky Blue, but she still supports her hometown club, Norwich City

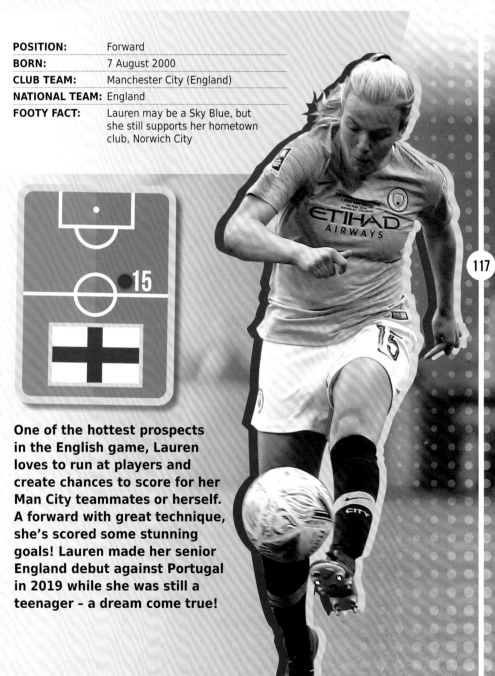

One of the hottest prospects in the English game, Lauren loves to run at players and create chances to score for her Man City teammates or herself. A forward with great technique, she's scored some stunning goals! Lauren made her senior England debut against Portugal in 2019 while she was still a teenager - a dream come true!

JORDYN HUITEMA

A Canadian attacker who plays her club football in France

POSITION:	Forward
BORN:	8 May 2001
CLUB TEAM:	Paris Saint-Germain (France)
NATIONAL TEAM:	Canada
FOOTY FACT:	Jordyn signed for one of France's top club sides just days after she turned 18

23

118

Standing tall at almost six feet, striker Jordyn is one of the youngest players ever to be called up for Canada at the age of just 15. She now stars alongside legend Christine Sinclair and was a part of Canada's squad for the 2019 World Cup. Jordyn has put plans to go to university on hold, instead choosing to sign a contract with PSG in France as a pro footballer.

LAUREN JAMES

A fearless young talent who scores goals wherever she plays!

POSITION:	Midfielder/Forward
BORN:	29 September 2001
CLUB TEAM:	Manchester United (England)
NATIONAL TEAM:	England U-19
FOOTY FACT:	Lauren's big brother Reece made his debut for Chelsea in 2019

Lauren moved from Arsenal's academy to help Manchester United win promotion in 2019, scoring 17 goals in her first season with the Red Devils. Strong and athletic, Lauren is a great finisher. One of the brightest young strikers in the league, she made history by scoring Man United's first-ever goal in the WSL.

ELLIE ROEBUCK

This Sky Blues stopper is playing for keeps!

POSITION:	Goalkeeper
BORN:	23 September 1999
CLUB TEAM:	Manchester City (England)
NATIONAL TEAM:	England
FOOTY FACT:	Ellie gets goalkeeping tips in training from Man City men's number 1, Ederson!

120

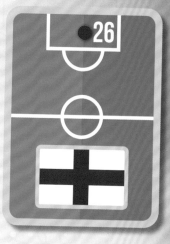

Sheffield-born goalkeeper Ellie made a name for herself when City's number 1, Karen Bardsley, suffered an injury. Ellie's fine performances in goal helped City win two trophies that year and qualify for the Champions League. At international level, Ellie has already made her senior debut for the Lionesses, though faces tough competition for the keeper's jersey.

GEORGIA STANWAY

City's number 10 has already won tons of trophies!

POSITION:	Forward
BORN:	3 January 1999
CLUB TEAM:	Manchester City (England)
NATIONAL TEAM:	England
FOOTY FACT:	As a schoolgirl, Georgia had to travel two hours each way to train with her nearest club, Blackburn Rovers

Forward Georgia made her debut for Manchester City at the age of 16 and has since won the WSL, the FA Cup and the League Cup. She's now one of the first names on the team-sheet for her club thanks to her fantastic goal-scoring record. Georgia was the youngest outfield player in the Lionesses' World Cup senior squad and has captained England's youth sides, too.

ULTIMATE FAN QUIZ

Tackle this quiz to see how much you know about the beautiful game that is women's football. For an even tougher test, get a friend to ask the questions without the answer options!

1. WHEN WAS THE FIRST FIFA WOMEN'S WORLD CUP HELD?

A. 1990

B. 1991

C. 2001

2. WHO IS THE CURRENT CAPTAIN OF THE LIONESSES?

A. Lucy Bronze

B. Steph Houghton

C. Jordan Nobbs

A.   **B.**   **C.**

3. WHAT IS THE NAME OF THE TOP WOMEN'S LEAGUE IN ENGLAND?

A. The Women's Premier League..

B. The Women's Championship...

C. The Women's Super League...

4. WHAT IS THE NICKNAME OF THE UNITED STATES NATIONAL TEAM?

A. The Star-spangled Banners...

B. The Stars and Stripes...

C. The Lilywhites..

5. MARTA HAS SCORED MORE GOALS AT WORLD CUP TOURNAMENTS THAN ANY OTHER PLAYER. HOW MANY EXACTLY?

A. 11.......................

B. 17.......................

C. 18.......................

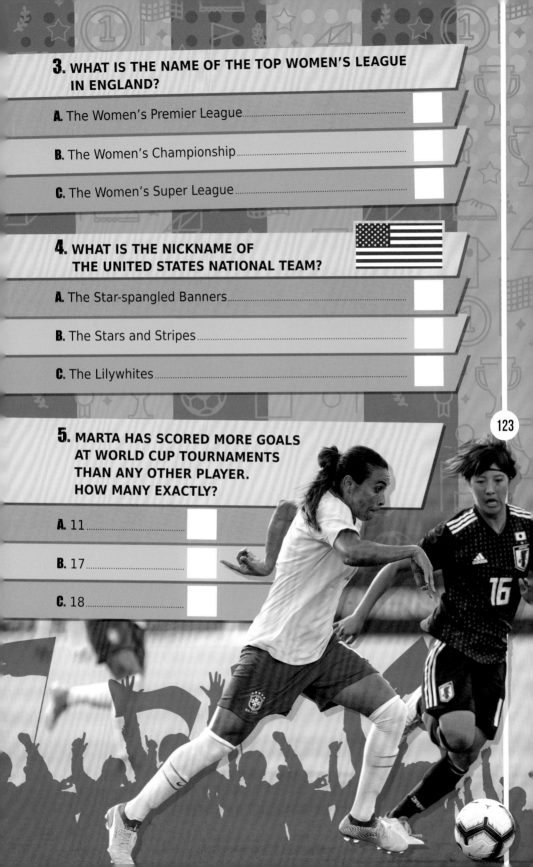

6. WHICH CLUB WON THE WSL IN THE 2018-19 SEASON?

A. Arsenal

B. Manchester City

C. Chelsea

7. WHICH COUNTRY WILL HOST THE UEFA WOMEN'S EURO 2021?

A. Russia

B. Spain

C. England

8. HOW MANY OLYMPIC FOOTBALL GOLD MEDALS HAVE THE UNITED STATES WON?

A. Four

B. Five

C. Seven

4

5

7

9. WHAT IS THE NICKNAME OF THE AUSTRALIAN WOMEN'S NATIONAL FOOTBALL TEAM?

A. The Socceroos..

B. The Mabels..

C. The Matildas..

10. WHAT NATIONALITY IS ARSENAL STRIKER VIVIANNE MIEDEMA?

A. French..

B. Norwegian..

C. Dutch...

ANSWERS

1 - B; 2 - B; 3 - C; 4 - B; 5 - B; 6 - A; 7 - C; 8 - C; 9 - A; 10 - C.

The final whistle blows! Now check your answers below and add up how many you got right to reveal your score.

0–3 CORRECT ANSWERS
FAIRWEATHER FAN!

More training is needed before you can call yourself a true fan of the women's game.

4–7 CORRECT ANSWERS
SUPER FAN!

What a performance! You've proved you know your footy.

8–10 CORRECT ANSWERS
NO. 1 FAN!

It's clear you're a champion fan – you love the beautiful game!

INDEX

PICTURE CREDITS

The publisher would like to thank the following sources for their kind permission to reproduce the pictures in this book.

t = top, c = centre, l = left, r = right

Alamy Stock Photo: 12-13 Alpha Stock; 14 ZUMA; 31, 40–41, 42–43, 96bl, 99t, 118 Alfo Co. Ltd; 33, 94, 113, 114 dpa picture alliance; 35, 72–73 Foto Arena LTDA; 51, 104, 122r PHC Images; 59 Pro Shots; 79, 115, 119 Action Foto Sport; 83 Cal Sport Media; 86 ZUMA Press; 87, 89, 91, 92, 93 Jonathan Larsen/Diadem Images; 88 PCN Photography; 90 imageBROKER; 95, 106, 107 Xinhua; 112 SPP Sport Press Photo; 117 Andrew Orchard Sports Photography; 120 Action Plus Sports Images.

COVER: Getty Images: l Michael Regan – FIFA; c Pat Elmont – FIFA; r David Ramos – FIFA.

Shutterstock: 6t, 7, 21l, 21r, 29, 37, 45, 46–47, 49, 53, 61, 62–63, 65, 68–69, 74–75, 97t, 103, 108, 121, 122c Jose Breton, Pics Action; 10–11 Utd. STUDIO; 15, 21lc, 21rc, 27, 54–55, 70t, 70–71, 105, 108–109, 122l Romain Biard; 17 Monkey Business Images; 24–25 Antonio Scorza; 39, 57, 80–81, 99b Oleksandr Osipov; 66–67 sirtravelalot; 70b, 116 Ververidis Vasilis; 76b, 76–77, 78–79, 98–99 Jason Ilagan; 81, 102 katatonia82; 84–85 Roka Pics; 96tr, 123 Lev Radin; 96–97 Action Sports Photography; 100–101 Fotokostic; 110–111 Alex Kravtsov.